The Job
of the
Planning
Commissioner

The Job of the Planning Commissioner

Third Edition

Revised

Albert Solnit

PLANNERS PRESS
AMERICAN PLANNING ASSOCIATION
WASHINGTON, D.C.
CHICAGO, ILLINOIS

Copyright 1987 by the American Planning Association
1313 E. 60th St., Chicago, IL 60637
ISBN 0-918286-51-4
Library of Congress Catalog Number 87-71171

Printed in the United States of America

Contents

To Marge, who missed many a Canadian sunset
preparing the manuscript.

Preface

Albert Sindlinger did a poll in Swarthmore, Pennsylvania. Every afternoon a battery of pollsters sat at a bank of telephones and called people all across the land. "What's the principal sickness in America today, ignorance or apathy?" "I don't know and I don't care," was the majority answer.
— Edward Bennett Williams in *National Observer,*
March 20, 1977

Men have always found it easy to be governed. What is hard is for them to govern themselves.
— Max Lerner

One of the unique things about America is the tradition of citizens serving in local government. One looks in vain for another country where the management of local affairs is not permanently placed in the hands of a national ministry of bureaucrats or provincial party hacks. In America, residents have been coming forward to give their time and common sense in unpaid service to their hometowns since 1620. Membership on planning commissions and other citizens' advisory boards is a continuation of a tradition that began in the town meetings of the first settlers.

When the first edition of this book was written, money for planning and other local government functions was far easier to come by than it is now. On the surface things certainly look darker today. Gone are the generous grants for "doing a plan"; wonderful abstractions like "New Frontier," "Great Society," and "New Federalism" to cheer for; and the belief that tomorrow will bring solutions to all of today's problems. In days past, the economy was perceived as an ever-growing pie that would provide everyone with bigger slices in the always rosy future. Thus, planners could get away with drawing up plans for lavish public facilities and amenities with no indication of the costs of acquiring and maintaining them.

Today we're learning to insist on knowing what things cost. We're also learning in most communities that we can and must do without some of the facilities and services that were taken for granted in the sixties and seventies. The benefit of this new outlook is not only that it forces plans and planners to look reality in the face but also that it inhibits mortgaging the future, as several big cities did in that era.

On the other hand, it's easy to overuse hindsight and forget that the generation of optimism and abundance produced hard-won gains in areas like environmental quality, conservation of resources such as forests and farmlands, expansion of housing opportunities, mass transit and highway systems, and the defense of livability in places that still have it. The job of planning commissioners in the eighties will be to consolidate and defend those gains in every city, county, and region in which their influence and advice can be felt.

Even though planning is in a period of retrenchment, the central beliefs that support the American way of planning are more evident than ever. These beliefs are also the reason for involving planning commissioners in the planning process. They are listed here.

a. **Citizen involvement:** Goals are best set by public discussion, and government should be open and accountable to the public in every step of the planning process. In many instances the commission acts as a surrogate public, particularly on broad, long-range issues, where it conducts the public dialogue with full access to the pertinent information.

b. **Smaller is better:** Americans believe in a series of little governments. We have been increasingly put off with big government in recent years, especially its bureaucratic complexity. We favor diversity in the establishment of local standards and a homegrown flavor in our communities. We also cherish the opportunity to fight city hall when it might choose a flavor we don't like. Good commissioners know and can protect a community's sense of place. They not only provide an arena for the fighters of city hall, but they also can give them commonsense responses.

c. **We live in a market rather than a centrally planned system:** In America, the market system is supreme, and shortcomings in the system are corrected by regulation and reform rather than by revolution or repression. We ask that our governments encourage economic activity rather than establish or replace it. Ideally, commissioners should have some firsthand experience with the workings of the marketplace. If not, they should at least grasp the fundamentals of taking risks, borrowing funds, and other financial dealings so that they can balance public and private interests with fairness and common sense.

d. **Orderly growth:** Planning in the United States has as one of its principal aims orderly, efficient, and timely development with the provision of adequate public services and facilities for it. Often this implies bargaining about allocations (e.g., zoning, permit approvals, and sewer and water hookups and extensions) among conflicting groups. Our belief is that such arbitration is best done as close to home as possible by people we know and can trust. Good commissioners have public trust as arbiters of such conflicts by being able to afford the kind of impartiality and nonpartisanship that politicians by their very calling can never hope to achieve.

This edition introduces several new chapters not only to update the earlier editions but also to sharpen the focus on how commissioners and their staffs can operate under these principles. The book continues to cover the basics that a newly appointed commissioner should absorb before the first meeting. Commissioners with more experience will benefit from using the book as a source of new ideas on how to better organize their work, to gain a fuller understanding of the whys as well as the how-tos of their tasks, and to learn how to improve themselves as the people charged with the stewardship of their community's future.

Introduction to the Revised Edition

We who try to solve problems in local communities are pretty much alone now. The focus of the Federal government in the late eighties has shifted away from helping alleviate local problems to deficits, drugs and defense. Decay of U.S. industry deficits in trade have moved the U.S. ever closer to becoming a raw materials plantation for the Japanese, while drugs have become a social as well as an economic drain. Increasingly local police, jails and courts are unable to even make a symbolic gesture at containing the problem, yet local and state crime costs are skyrocketing year after year. As for defense, Seymour Melman pointed out: The guns or butter choice once consigned to a timeless future can no longer be ignored for the "long run" is now, and the nation cannot have it both ways, as the accompanying sample of trade offs generated by the administrations' budgets (fiscal 1986) illustrates.

Proposed cut in funds for mass transit system	- $2.8 billion -	Navy (EA6B) airplane program for surveillance and communications jamming.
Proposed cuts in housing for the elderly and handicapped and the cut in energy assistance for poor people.	- $1.5 billion -	One projected (LHD-1) Marine amphibious assault ship.
Proposed elimination of the Federal share of a 15 year national plan for sewage treatment to meet minimum Clean Water Act standards.	- $30 billion -	The Navy's Aegis (CG-47) cruiser program.
Mayor Koch's 10 year plan for repairing New York City's infrastructure.	- $40.6 billion -	The stealth radar evading bomber program.
Federal funds needed by Connecticut for rebuilding bridges and roads.	- $3.7 billion -	1986 planned research and development for . . . (Star Wars) program.
Annual additional funding to abate deterioration in Federal, state, and local public facilities.	- $18 billion -	three nuclear-powered aircraft carriers with their planes and support ships, plus the Navy's antisubmarine airplane (P-36) program.

Estimated cost of cleaning up 10,000 toxic-waste dumps that contaminate the nation's soil and water.	- $100 billion -	The Navy's Trident II submarine and F-18 jet fighter programs.
Estimated cost of renovating an average five room medium income Manhattan West Side apartment.	- $42,287 -	One (F-16 jet fighter) antenna puller tool; one antenna alignment tool; one antenna puller height gauge; one antenna hexagon wrench.

In this climate, the job of representing the people who aren't here yet and the young people who will inhabit our mortgaged future is going to become increasingly difficult. In many communities, not only is no one home, but the lights aren't even on anymore, when considerations of the future are raised in council chambers or county hearing rooms.

It is hoped that this book will help readers put the future back in planning decisions and at least some illumination on long range considerations.

Albert Solnit
1987

What Are These Amateurs Doing in Government?

1

I know of no safe depository of the ultimate powers of society but the people themselves; and if we think them not enlightened enough to exercise their control with a wholesome discretion, the remedy is not to take it from them but to inform their discretion by education.

— Thomas Jefferson

As a planning commissioner, you've probably been so busy at your unpaid job that you can hardly remember how you felt the day you were asked if you'd serve. Perhaps you may recall feeling a little uncertain, thinking, "What do I know about planning and zoning laws and subdivisions and all that complex stuff they're always writing up in the paper?" Perhaps the real reason you decided to sacrifice all those hours of after-work time to your community is that **planning is too important to be left to the professional planners**. Someone with roots in the community and common sense had better be around to listen to the people and help direct the community's planning and growth toward where they want it to go. Mr. Justice Louis Brandeis put it this way:

Since government is not an exact science, prevailing public opinion concerning the evils and the remedy is among the important facts deserving consideration; particularly when the public conviction is both deep-seated and widespread and has been reached with deliberation.

In other words, the art of good planning lies not so much with the techniques employed as with the purposes for which plans are carried out. Someone who can serve the long-range interests of a community, unbound by election promises, political expediency, or narrow interests is the definition of the good planning

1

commissioner. In theory, you're essential to democratic local government. Your roots in government can be traced all the way back to the New England town meetings of colonial times. Most of the nineteenth century has to be viewed as the Dark Ages of citizen involvement in community building. Not until the muckrakers, late in the 1800s, exposed the shameful slums into which callous robber baron landlords had crammed millions of the urban poor was the public again convinced that it had to assume responsibility for the condition of housing and sanitation in American cities and towns.

The beginning of the twentieth century saw many U.S. cities under "boss" rule, characterized by political machines for the production of graft through the provision of contracts and franchises for street paving and water, sewer, and trolley lines. In the teens and twenties, a reform movement swept many of these corrupt bosses out of power and replaced them with nonpartisan city council-manager forms of government. Even so, councilmen were still viewed as "politicians" and as such were not to be trusted. Planning and zoning commissions of appointed citizens were thus created as quasi-independent bodies to insulate planning from the "dirtiness of politics." Edward M. Bassett, co-author of the seminal 1928 City Planning Enabling Act, said as late as 1938 that the master plan of a community "should be kept within the four walls of the city planning commission." This view is still common.

Another major antecedent of today's planning commission was the City Beautiful Movement of 1890-1910. Stimulated by the eclectic grandeur of the 1893 Chicago Exposition, this movement resulted in a nationwide rash of public monument building in the form of palatial city halls, grand boulevards, and colossal floodlit fountains. While indifferent to pressing social and functional needs, this movement did lay the groundwork for comprehensive planning by stressing three dimensions in contrast to the earlier two-dimensional U.S. town planning by lot plat and street layout. The movement also typically included the appointment of a blue-ribbon panel of local citizens, and the hiring of an eminent consultant (usually an architect or landscape architect) to draw up a one-shot city plan for them so as to enhance civic grandeur. These elements of the movement foreshadowed the current citizen planning commission and the consultant-prepared plan.

It was soon realized that these plans should be placed under some kind of public authority. In 1913, Massachusetts led the way by making it mandatory for all cities of more than 10,000 people to create official planning boards. State after state followed this lead, and as zoning was instituted around the nation lawyers also became planning commission consultants.

In these early days, the commission leadership was usually drawn from the chamber of commerce and the well-to-do elements of the town, which helps explain the fact that the major goal of these commissions was the stabilization and protection of property values. This was done by segregating public nuisances and incompatible use out of "good" residential areas. At the same time, areas that had a potential for speculative profit outside of the established good residential areas were consistently overzoned for commercial, industrial, and multifamily uses. While plans were still being prepared, the gap between what was in the plans and what got zoned and built led planner Norton Long to label master plans "the civic New Year's resolution."

In the thirties, commission concerns expanded from civic aesthetics and zoning to engineering functions such as the width and alignment of streets and the location and adequacy of public facilities and utilities. These new interests soon led to concern for efficient government spending and operations, which led to the commissions' becoming involved in capital budgeting.

The great postwar impetus to planning commission activity was section 701 of the Housing Act of 1954, which funneled federal money to local jurisdictions to cover two-thirds or more of the costs of preparing plans, studies, and surveys. Staffs, agencies, and consultants for the commissions grew in proportion to the money available.

As the nation passed into the troubled sixties, many more new issues forced their way onto the typical planning commission's agenda. These included social welfare considerations (housing and racial issues), environmental impacts, design controls, historic preservation, urban renewal, and most recently growth controls. The latest change for planning commissioners has been that their historic emphasis on efficient regulation and processing of new development has been called into question by a new mood of the seventies. Planning has traditionally been growth oriented, yet many communities are now faced with a new set of problems due to "decline"—especially those in the Northeast and Midwest. In the suburbs, it is no longer just a question of where to put new growth as it comes in but whether to have it all, while paradoxically the central cities and older communities search for the means to halt further decline and decay.

Moreover, for some time a number of the best and brightest professional critics of local government planning have concluded that you and your fellow lay-citizen planning commissioners are not only a waste of everyone's time but, worse yet, a redundant obstacle to getting governmental action. As one small-town mayor confided to me, "Our planning commission raises so much fuss about everything that we only have them around because we're legally required to. I try to listen to any item that's been through them on its own merits."

More erudite commission eliminators have advanced the following arguments for the abolition of your job as commissioner:

a. **The commission's advice is merely lay opinion.** The legislative body not only has the final say but also has access to the same technical staff and will probably hear the same testimony from developers and the public; so why should planning matters suffer from duplicate deliberation and delay?

b. **The general plan**, as technically interpreted by a professional staff, should be the policy guide for city councils, boards of supervisors, and other local legislators. Since the plan is a legally adopted document and the commissioners are merely appointed amateurs, following the plan rather than the commission comes closest to following the rules of law rather than rules of men.

c. **Commissioners are not directly responsible to the people through the electoral process** and thus they contravene the democratic process when they try to form goals and policy independently of elected officials.

d. **The planning commission is wrongfully set up as a nonpolitical buffer to shield planners and planning from the heat of political controversy.** Therefore, this argument concludes, the planning commission is just an anachronistic holdover from the reform days of the twenties when politicians were not to be trusted and planning affairs were to be kept untainted by politics.

Some counterarguments to these anticommission propositions are as follows:

a. **The commission is merely lay opinion:** The commission should be transmitting much more than lay opinions to a legislative body. A properly functioning commission serves in somewhat the same way as the legislative committees in Congress or the state capital in that it evaluates information from staff and testimony in hearings for the purpose of making recommendations to guide legislative action. In so doing, the commission acts as an extension of the local legislative body to conduct the necessary profound study and inquiry into various planning affairs for which a busy five- to seven-person city council simply couldn't find the time. The commission carrying out this function should serve as a feedback mechanism to inform the elected officials about what people feel and want in community planning and where the community's best long-range interests lie.

b. **The general plan, not the commission, should guide planning policy:** It is generally agreed that the general plan has to be constantly restudied and revised in the light of changing conditions. This is particularly important since the recent reawakening of the courts' interest in the relationship of planning to land use regulations. The courts have been reacting adversely to ad hoc decision making with increasing vigor. Coupled with this is the recent growth of environmental concern that demands a planning process that will select and build on those alternatives that are the least destructive to the environment. Thus the Oregon Supreme Court found in *Baker v. City of Milwaukee* (1975) that, since the city had adopted a plan, it was required to zone in accordance with that plan so that the plan would not be frustrated. The Court ruled that the plan, as a "constitutional document for land-use planning, [is] superior to zoning regulations." (California's legislature has followed suit by requiring that zoning ordinances be consistent with general plans.)

So now the general plan must be considered an impermanent constitution for the future growth of a city or county. It's impermanent because this process requires continual effort to stay relevant. As a practical matter, a city council is usually too busy to work long enough with a planning staff or consultant in the restudy, discussion, and hearings needed to do the job

5

properly. More important, professional planners need a client close at hand to give them feedback on their proposals in the form of local preferences. Thus, while the legislative body may be the client who pays the bills, the commissioners should be the chief client. "The reason," as the pioneer planner John Howard said, "is to keep plans from being hatched and kept in a vacuum." In communities without a planning staff, a commission allows the public to get more of its money's worth from consultants, because the commission has the time and incentive to absorb what they have to offer.

Furthermore, in interpreting a plan, a planning director often can't withstand the pressures brought by other department heads or the chief administrator, who want favorable findings (or silence) about their pet project's conformity with the plan. Since the commission is not subordinate to these people, it is able to withstand the pressures that the planner may bend to and thus the commission can allow the planner to hand up professional advice in a safer climate. Even when there isn't a planning staff, the commission can act more objectively than the building inspector, public works engineer, or whoever is responsible for the staff planning function.

c. **Commissions contravene the democratic process:** Obviously legislative officials should establish policy and direction, but much of the time they need some nudging. Generating ideas and calling attention to needs for policy direction are excellent ways to do this, assuming that the commission has the legislators' ears and respect.

d. **Commissions are an obsolete holdover to shield planning and professional planners from politics:** While there may have been some truth to this charge in the distant past, today most good planning commissioners are up to their hips in politics. There's no way of appearing neutral when you have to make a decision on a controversial matter at least once in every meeting. Moreover, the commission should not be the planner's shield but the best indicator of how he's performing his job, because it uses his products, sees him in action consistently, and is the first to know how he's regarded in the community. Administrators, on the other hand, may be the planner's bosses on an organization chart; but typically an administrator is more interested in how a planner keeps house, prepares budgets, supervises personnel, and keeps the enemy out of the administrator's camp.

In addition to these functions, a good planning commission has many other functions that justify its existence. A few of the most important are:

a. A planning commission is a splendid training ground for future officeholders. The one in my town has graduated knowledgeable people familiar with the major problems of government into council seats for years, and it continues to do so. Experienced commissioners also make fine civic leaders, because they've taken the heat on major public issues. They've not only made tough decisions; if they've done their job properly, they've established clear grounds for those decisions.

b. A planning commission that is doing its job is looking into the "futurity" (defined by Peter Drucker as the impact that actions taken now will have on the future) of the actions that may be taken in contrast to most elected officials, whose long-range concerns may not extend beyond the next election. A corollary to this concern for the future that marks the good commission is respect and awareness for the traditions and heritage of the past. In many communities the image of the place is projected by the irreplaceable structures and spaces of earlier times. A good commission should be and has been the community's first line of defense against mindless visual pollution and destruction of the values of the past.

c. The good commission, having no political axes to grind, can work toward consensus solutions for problems requiring a lot of technical study, and can send up an objective course of action that the more politicized elected officials might never evolve.

d. When politically "hot" issues arise, the commission can and should act as a lightning rod to draw out and clarify the positions of people on all sides of a question. Once this is done, the politicians upstairs can more safely and rationally make "statesmanlike" decisions.

e. It has been widely held that the commissioners, rather than the council members or supervisors, are a better group for achieving intergovernmental cooperation, such as joint planning with school districts, utilities, and neighboring jurisdictions. This is because commissioners are not authorized to (and should not) fly the flag of local sovereignty or elected authority or carry on the manipulative pushing and pulling that characterize "playing politics."

f . A good commission has the power to command public attention. Therefore the objective recommendations it sends up to the elected officials have the power to forestall arbitrary, capricious, and ad hoc decision making being covered up with rhetoric and double talk. It is extremely important to keep in mind that the commission's one real source of power stems from the requirement that the legislative body must seek its advice. To the extent that this advice is logical, clear, and well thought out, it will bear witness in public against other actions that would allow expediency and special privilege to rule.

In most states, the existence of a planning commission is a matter of law. None of these laws insures that a planning commission will be worthwhile. Only the people who become planning commissioners can do this.

Understanding the Language of Planning and Zoning

2

When I use a word, Humpty Dumpty said . . . , it means just what I choose it to mean—neither more nor less.
                    —Lewis Carroll
                    Through the Looking-Glass

Pity the new commissioner listening in to the shoptalk of his or her colleagues and hearing something like this: "It was only an accessory use in an interim zone, so while it could have gone through variance procedures with the zoning administrator, we're going to handle it as a nonconforming use because it violates the setback requirements and encroaches on right-of-way, and so we can require that it be removed by amortization of the use."

Some commissioners never recover from overhearing snatches of conversation like this and retreat into their shells, never to emerge as participating members of the group.

Many people who come into a group dealing with the terminology of planning and zoning are often as unable to handle the "language barrier" as a traveler in a foreign country. The following terms[1] are among the most commonly used in planning commission work over the years. An understanding of their meaning should allow the new commissioner to communicate with planners, zoning administrators, and veteran commissioners without resorting to sign language or drawing pictures.

[1] A number of the terms and their definitions in this chapter have been adapted from Charles Abrams, *The Language of Cities* (New York: Avon Books, 1971), perhaps the best overall guide to the speech of planners, developers, realtors, and others who create the jargon of building and land-use regulation.

Abandonment: A situation where a residential building is abandoned by its owner. There are two typical situations in which this occurs. The first is the case of an old apartment building requiring extensive and costly renovations and occupied by poor families who cannot pay higher rent to recompense the owner for the renovations. The second is the case of the single-family home financed under federal mortgage insurance programs and abandoned because of inability to pay or because of poor quality, with lending institutions and builders profiting and the government and taxpayer losing. In either case abandonment leads to a cycle of further deterioration, vacancies, and vandalism. A mortgagee is often unwilling to foreclose, in situations where mortgages are not insured, because foreclosure in such a situation may simply mean assumption of the unprofitable dilemma from which the owner has fled. After a number of years of the owner's failure to pay taxes, the city may be forced to foreclose and thus inherit the problem. In the case of insured mortgages, HUD assumes ultimate responsibility.

Accessory use: An activity or structure incidental or secondary to the principal use on the same site.

Aesthetic zoning: The regulation of building design and site developments in the interest of appearance. "... It is within the power of the legislature to determine that the community should be beautiful as well as healthy," said Mr. Justice William O. Douglas in delivering the majority decision in *Berman* v. *Parker.*

Air rights: The right to use the air space over the property of someone else, typically over railways and highways. With modern materials and acoustical treatment, the use of air rights in such a situation can create extensive building space where none seems to exist. The necessary engineering usually requires that the building be a major structure in both size and cost. The Prudential Center, built over the Massachusetts Turnpike in Boston, is an example of the use of air rights.

Amortization: A term used in zoning to mean the process by which nonconforming uses and structures must be discontinued or made to conform to requirements of the ordinance at the end of a specified period of time. The term itself is a bastardization of the real estate term by which borrowers are required to pay back a debt in regular payments over a fixed period of time, e.g., installment payments on the principal on a mortgage.

Provisions for amortizing nonconformities are included in a number of zoning ordinances but seldom are enforced except in the case of such low-value use as signs.

Architectural control: Regulations and procedures requiring structures to be suitable, harmonious, and in keeping with the general appearance, historical character, or style of their surrounding area. Critics have suggested that architectural controls legislate "taste" and require "new antiques" in historical zones, thereby cheapening the real landmarks. Defenders point out that a community that has a historical character or prevailing architectural design should protect and preserve it from the cheap and vulgar, most particularly from building packages of national chains of fast food franchises, filling stations, or others whose trademark is the flashy and sleazy building and sign.

Bonuses (also known as incentive zoning): The awarding of bonus credits to a development in the form of allowing more intensive use of the land if such public benefits as greater than the minimum open space are preserved, special provisions for low- and moderate-income housing are made, or public plazas and courts are provided at ground level.

Buffer zone: A strip of land created to separate and protect one type of land use from another; for example, as a screen of planting or fencing to insulate the surroundings from the noise, smoke, or visual aspects of an industrial zone or junkyard.

Building area: The total square footage of a lot covered by a building measured on a horizontal plane at mean grade level, exclusive of uncovered porches, terraces, and steps.

Building code: Regulations governing building design, construction, and maintenance. They are based on the government's police power to protect the health, safety, and welfare of the public. Policies vary in different cities and within cities so far as enforcement is concerned. Codes may not be enforced in whole areas because it is impractical to do so. The need for enforcement, however, may suddenly be raised as justification for a project. In other cases, code requirements may be written so that they discourage rehabilitation, by making it too expensive, and this encourages deterioration and eventual clearance and rebuilding.

Building envelope: The net cubic space that remains for placing a structure on a site after building line, setback, side yard, height, and bulk regulations are observed.

Building line: A building limit fixed at a specific distance from the front or side boundaries of a lot beyond which a structure cannot lawfully extend.

Bulk regulations: Zoning or other regulations that by controlling the height, mass, density, and location of buildings set a maximum limit on the intensity of development so as to provide proper light, air, and open space.

Capital improvement program: A governmental timetable of permanent improvements budgeted to fit fiscal capability some years into the future. A local planning commission is sometimes given authority to develop and review the capital improvement program, thereby linking planning to the annual budgeting process. Capital improvement programs are usually projected five or six years in advance and should be updated annually.

Carrying capacity: The level of land use or human activity that can be permanantly accommodated without an irreversible change in the quality of air, water, land, or plant and animal habitats. In human settlements, this term also refers to the upper limits beyond which the quality of life, community character, or human health, welfare, and safety will be impaired.

Certificate of compliance: This term has two distinctly different meanings in different places. (1) It is commonly used synonymously with a zoning permit in which an official certifies that the plans for a proposed use are in conformance with the zoning ordinance. (2) In a second, much less commonly used application, the term means an enforcement device which, in reference to a certain class of structure (usually multiple-family dwellings), incorporates in one document an indication of conformance, or lack thereof, with the several municipal codes—zoning, building, housing, occupancy—which may apply to a specific property. This latter certificate puts prospective purchasers on notice that the property may be nonconforming or in actual violation of local codes and what must be done to achieve compliance. It also helps considerably in code administration and enforcement. It is only in use in a few places.

Cluster development (or zoning): A type of development that allows the reduction of lot sizes below the zoning ordinance's minimum requirements if the land thereby gained is preserved as permanent open space for the community. Often the developer will try to offer as open space the unbuildable lands, i.e., the very steep gullies and ravines that were left over from the building process on the site.

Code enforcement: The attempt by a government unit to cause property owners and others responsible for buildings and related land to bring their properties up to standards required by building codes, housing codes, and other ordinances. Code enforcement, used rigorously and continuously, can be a prime instrument in arresting urban deterioration.

Combination zone: Zones which are superimposed over other zones and which either add further requirements or replace certain requirements of the underlying zone. They are a form of overlay zone except that they normally are wholly within other zones and may apply to only parts of zones. Buffer zones, where a higher intensity zone abuts one of lower intensity, may be applied as combination zones. In Los Angeles, for example, the ordinance provides for the following combination zones: airport approach, conservation, design review, equestrian, hillside, mobile home, general planned development, and scenic reservation.

Community facilities: Public or privately owned facilities used by the public, such as streets, schools, libraries, parks, and playgrounds; also facilities owned and operated by nonprofit private agencies such as churches, settlement houses, and neighborhood associations.

Compatibility: The characteristics of different uses or activities that permit them to be located near each other in harmony and without conflict. It is a general but important concept which forms the basis for the segregation of uses, through zoning, in districts. The designation of permitted and special-permit uses in a zoning district is intended to achieve compatibility within the district. Performance standards, which measure compatibility more closely, are beginning to replace the less precise and less flexible use lists in many locations. Some elements affecting compatibility include: intensity of occupancy as measured by dwelling units per acre; floor area ratio; pedestrian or vehicular traffic generated; volume of goods handled; and such environmental effects as noise, vibration, glare, air pollution, or radiation. On the other hand, many aspects of compatibility are based on personal preference and are much harder to measure quantitatively, at least for regulatory purposes.

Condemnation: The taking of private property by a government unit for public use, when the owner will not relinquish it through sale or other means; the owner is recompensed by payment of "market value." The power to take the property is based on the concept of "eminent domain." Condemnation is used to acquire property for street widenings, parks, and other purposes. The term "to condemn" a building is used to indicate determination by a government agency that a building is unfit for use because it is structurally or otherwise unsafe or unhealthy.

Conditional rezoning: The attachment of special conditions to a rezoning which are not spelled out in the text of the ordinance. Along with other devices to assure compliance, it may bind the developer to the conditions through filing a covenant. While frequently invalidated by the courts, its recent legal history has been more favorable. Conditional rezoning is considered to be a form of contract zoning and therefore is often found illegal by the courts. The distinction between conditional zoning and contract zoning is fuzzy and seems to revolve around which is emphasized more, the conditions or the contract.

Conditional use: A use that may locate in certain zoning districts provided it will not be detrimental to the public health, morals, and welfare and will not impair the integrity and character of the zoned district. Examples of conditional use permitted in a commercial, industrial, or agricultural zone are

14

temporary carnivals, religious revivals, and rock concerts. The duty of the commission approving such applications is to condition the use so that it will not be unsuitable to the surrounding area or community at large.

Condominium: The legal arrangement in which a dwelling unit in an apartment building or residential development is individually owned but in which the common areas are owned, controlled, and maintained through an organization consisting of all the individual owners. Condominium ownership provides design flexibility and the sharing of responsibility through the use of common open spaces that are in addition to private open spaces.

Conservation easement: A tool for acquiring open space with less than full-fee purchase; the public agency buys only certain specific rights from the owner. These may be positive rights, giving the public rights to hunt, fish, hike, or ride over the land, or they may be restricted rights limiting the uses to which the owner may put the land in the future. Scenic easements allow the public agency to use the owner's land for scenic enhancement such as roadside landscaping and vista point preservation.

Conversion: The partitioning of a single-dwelling unit into two or more separate households or the conversion of the use of an existing building into another use. "Bootleg conversion" is a common term for an illegal conversion of a structure.

Cooperative: A group of dwellings or an apartment building that is jointly owned by the residents, the common ownership including the open space and all other parts of the property. The purchase of stock entitles the buyer to sole occupancy but not the individual ownership of a specified unit. Like the condominium, the cooperative arrangement offers certain flexibilities in design and economies in development and maintenance.

Cost benefit analysis: An approach to evaluating the advantages and disadvantages of a project, policy, action, etc., in which an attempt is made to quantify the various results, so that the pros and cons can more objectively be compared with one another. At its best, the approach achieves a simplified way of looking at complex issues. At its worst, it imposes a false "objectivity" by giving erroneous dollar value or other numerical value to such matters as attitudes, visual quality, and other concerns that resist quantification.

Dedication: A turning over of private land for a public use by an owner or developer, and its acceptance for such use by the governmental agency in charge of the public function for which it will be used. Dedications for roads, parks, school sites, or other public uses are often made conditions for the approval of a development by a planning commission.

Dedication, payment in lieu of: Cash payments required as a substitute for a dedication of land by an owner or developer, usually at so many dollars per lot. This overcomes the two principal problems of land-dedication requirements by applying the exactions on development more equitably and by allowing purchase of sites at the best locations rather than merely in places where the development is large enough to be required to dedicate a school or park. (This is not legal in all states.)

Density, control of: A limitation on the occupancy of land. Density can be controlled through zoning by one method or a combination of following methods: use restrictions, e.g., single- or multiple-family dwellings; minimum lot-size require- ments; floor area ratio; land-use-intensity zoning; setback and yard requirements; minimum house-size requirements; ratios between the number and types of housing units and land area; direct limitations on units per acre; requirements for lot area per dwelling unit; and other means. The major distinction between different residential districts often is in their allowable density.

Density transfer: A technique of retaining open space by concentrating residential densities, usually in compact areas adjacent to existing urbanization and utilities, with outlying areas being left open, so that the residential density of the entire community will average out at the same number of dwelling units as if the community were developed from end to end with large lots. A variation of this involves allowing density transfers by private developers who buy the development rights of outlying properties that are publicly desirable for open space and adding the additional density to the base

16

number of units permitted in the zone in which they propose to develop.

Development rights: A broad range of less-than-fee-simple ownership interests, mainly referring to easements. Thus, an owner can retain complete or absolute (fee simple) rights to land and sell the development rights to another. The owner would keep title but agree to continue using the land as it had been used in the past, with the right to develop resting in the holder of the development rights. Such rights usually are expressed in terms of the density allowed under the existing zoning. In transfer of development rights, the amount may not exceed the difference between this total and that which actually exists on a given parcel of land, expressed in dwelling units per acre or square feet of building area.

Some jurisdictions have developed programs to acquire development rights in order to keep land open. These programs were originated because it was felt that total public ownership was undesirable and typically infeasible politically. The purchase of only selected rights would be substantially less expensive than total purchase and would still allow the owner to continue making economic use of his or her land. In practice, though, public acquisition of development rights has often cost up to 95 percent of the full market value of the land.

Downzoning: A change in the zoning classification of land to a classification permitting development that is less intensive or dense, such as from multifamily to single-family or from commercial or industrial to residential. A change in the opposite direction is called "upzoning."

Due process at law: Generally, a requirement that legal proceedings be carried out in accordance with established rules and principles. Commonly, it takes two forms: procedural and substantive. Procedural due process means an assurance that all parties to a proceeding are treated fairly and equally, that citizens have a right to have their views heard, that necessary information is available for informed opinions to be developed, that conflicts of interest are avoided, and that, generally, the appearance of, as well as the fact of, corruption does not exist. Procedural due process requirements are increasingly being imposed by the legislatures and the courts in proceedings involving zoning changes, whether performed

17

by an administrative agency or official—such as a board of adjustment or hearing examiner—or by legislative bodies—such as city councils—when they perform essentially administrative functions like rezoning small parcels or approving floating zone applications.

The meaning of substantive due process is less precise, but it usually refers to the payment by government of "just compensation" to property owners when their property is condemned by government or is severely diminished in value because of government action.

Easement: Usually the right to use property owned by another for specific purposes. Utility companies often have easements on the private property of individuals for utility facilities and maintenance access. Another common form of easement and one which can lend design flexibility to a project is an access easement for purposes of pedestrian and/or vehicular circulation.

Eminent domain: The right of a government to make a taking of private property for public use or benefit upon payment of just compensation to the owner. The terms "eminent domain" and "condemnation" are often used interchangeably, although condemnation may also mean the demolition by public authority of an unsafe structure where no compensation is paid to the owner and the condemned property does not become public land. "Inverse condemnation" is a condition in which the governmental use of police power to regulate the use of land is so severe that it represents a de facto taking of private property for public benefit or use without just compensation.

Environmental impact: An assessment of a proposed project or activity to determine whether it will have significant environmental effects on the natural and manmade environments. When no significant environmental impact will result, a "negative declaration" is submitted instead of the Environmental Impact Report (EIR) which is the detailed report on how the project will effect the environment. (An EIR may also be known as an Environmental Impact Statement or EIS.) Significant environmental effects are generally associated with those actions which:

1. Alter existing environmental components such as air and water quality, wildlife habitats, and food chains.
2. Disrupt neighborhood or community structure (i.e., displace low-income people).
3. Further threaten rare or endangered plant or animal species.
4. Alter or substantially disrupt the appearance or surroundings of a scenic, recreational, historical, or archaeological site.
5. Induce secondary effects such as changes in land use, unplanned growth, or traffic congestion.

Exaction: A contribution or payment required as an authorized precondition for receiving a development permit. It usually refers to mandatory dedication or fee in lieu of dedication requirements found in many subdivision regulations.

Exception (also called variance): The official provision of an exemption from compliance with the terms or conditions of a building or zoning regulation by a local board or administrator vested with the power to authorize it. It is usually granted if there are practical difficulties in meeting the existing requirements literally, or if the deviation or exception would not have a detrimental impact on adjacent properties or affect substantial compliance with the regulations. While an exception (or variance or special use) is a departure from the standard application of the zoning ordinance, it is provided for within the ordinance. A day-care center, for example, might not ordinarily be permitted in an area zoned exclusively residential, yet since this might be a perfectly desirable and acceptable place for the care of preschool children, allowance for an exception, subject to conditioning of how the operation will be conducted, will be preestablished in the text of the zoning ordinance.

Exclusionary zoning: Zoning which has the effect of keeping out a community racial minority, poor people, or in some cases, additional population of any kind. Techniques such as large-lot zoning or high floor area or minimum residential floor area requirements which increase housing costs have been challenged for their potential exclusionary effects. Similarly, discretionary techniques have been subject to challenge; they may permit a community to deny certain applications and conceal the real reasons. Exclusionary zoning, in all its subtle variations, is considered by many the most effective and pervasive tool used by suburbs to maintain their homogeneous character. A growing number of state court decisions are invalidating exclusionary practices, whether intentional or unintentional, and in some cases are requiring affirmative, inclusionary practices. On the other hand, discretionary techniques, such as inclusionary zoning, can be an important part of an inclusionary land-use program.

Externalities, side effects, spillovers, repercussion effects: The impacts on others than the direct beneficiaries or targets of a course of action. Externalities may be local or widespread and may be fiscal, environmental, social, or all three. Much of the recent environmental impact legislation is based on increased understanding of the spillovers of development processes on a community's natural and human environment.

Family: In many zoning ordinances the legal definition is a group of two or more persons related by blood, marriage, or adoption residing together; this is the basic occupancy intended for "single-family residence" districts. In recent years communes and other cooperative "lifestyle" arrangements of unrelated and mostly single individuals have run afoul of the single-family residence zone regulations that use this definition of the family (and a specific limit to how many "nonrelated" individuals may dwell together) to exclude such groups from dwelling in single-family residences.

Final subdivision map (or plat): A map of an approved sub-division filed in the county recorder's office. It usually shows surveyed lot lines, street rights of way, easements, monuments, and distances, angles, and bearings, pertaining to the exact dimensions of all parcels, street lines, and so forth.

Finding: A determination or conclusion based on the evidence presented and prepared by a hearings body in support of its decision. A zoning board of adjustment or governing body is usually required by law to hold a public hearing to hear evidence when it receives a petition for a variance, special permit, rezoning, or appeal of an administrative official's decision. When it presents its decision, the body is often required to demonstrate in writing that the facts presented in evidence support its decision in conformance with the law. If, for example, the law requires evidence of a hardship before a variance can be granted, the board of adjustment must support its approval by finding that a hardship, in fact, exists. A requirement to produce findings of fact is often found in due process rules of state legislation.

Floating zone (or design district): A zoning district that is described in the text of the zoning ordinance but not mapped as a specific district in a specific location. When a project of sufficient size anywhere within unrestricted areas can meet certain other requirements, however, the floating zone can be anchored and the area designated on the zoning map.

Floor area ratio (FAR): A formula for determining permitted building volume as a multiple of the area of the lot. For example, a ratio of six on a 5,000-square-foot lot would allow a three-story building with 10,000 square feet on each floor or a six-story building with 5,000 square feet on each floor or a variety of similar combinations as long as the total floor area did not exceed 30,000 square feet. Some zoning ordinances offer an incentive in the form of a higher FAR in order to reduce site coverage and thus encourage provision of plazas and other open spaces on the ground level.

General plan: A legal document often in the form of a map and accompanying text adopted by the local legislative body. The plan is a compendium of its general policies regarding the long-term development of its jurisdiction. It is also called a city plan, comprehensive plan, or master plan.

Growth management (growth control; land-use development management): The use by a community of a wide range of techniques in combination to permit it to determine its own amount, type, and rate of growth and to channel it into designated areas. Comprehensive plans often form the backbone of the system; devices used to execute growth management policy may include zoning, emphasizing flexibility, capital improvements, programming, adequate public facilities ordinances, urban limit lines, population caps or ceilings, and many others. Some of the sophisticated systems have departed dramatically from the traditional land-use controls, using a variety of innovative devices to achieve particular policies. Conceptually, growth management differs from conventional approaches in that it does not accept likely population growth and its rate as inevitable; these are open to question and are subject to determination by public policy and action.

Guidelines: An undetailed statement of policy direction around which specific details may be established later. In city planning this often takes the form of a local jurisdiction's adopting general principles, to which private development must conform, without mapping or describing the specific details of what may or may not be built or where (e.g., floating zone).

Highest and best use: The use of land in such a way that its development will bring maximum profit to the owner. It's a theoretical real estate concept that does not take into account the externalities from such a use of land, and thus public regulations often limit land use to some activity that will provide the owners with less than maximum profits in order to minimize spillover costs to other properties and the public at large. Thus the term is not commonly used in planning but is often heard at zoning hearings.

Houses, halfway: Therapeutic residences that provide a sheltered and transitional environment for persons emerging from mental or penal institutions or drug treatment centers. They are open and noninstitutional in order to help ease their residents' return to being fully functioning members of the community. When they are proposed for residential areas, a great deal of public controversy is likely to ensue, and many jurisdictions treat them as conditional uses in order to allay public fears.

Improved land: Raw land that has been improved with basic facilities such as roads, sewers, water lines, and other public infrastructure facilities in preparation for meeting development standards. It sometimes refers to land with buildings as well, but usually land with buildings and utilities would be called a developed area, while the term "improved land" more often describes vacant land with utilities only.

Infrastructure: Streets, water and sewer lines, and other public facilities necessary to the functioning of an urban area.

Interim or study zone: This is a zoning technique used to temporarily freeze development in an area until a permanent classification for it can be decided upon. It is generally used to preserve the status quo while an area or communitywide comprehensive plan is prepared to serve as a basis for permanent zoning.

Land-use plan: A basic element of a comprehensive plan, it designates the future use or reuse of the land within a given jurisdiction's planning area, and the policies and reasoning used in arriving at the decisions in the plan. The land-use plan serves as a guide to official decisions in regard to the distribution and intensity of private development, as well as public decisions on the location of future public facilities and open spaces. It is also a basic guide to the structuring of zoning and subdivision controls, urban renewal, and capital improvement programs.

Leapfrog development: Development that occurs well beyond the existing limits of urban development and thus leaves intervening vacant land behind. This bypassing of the next-in-line lands at the urban fringe results in the haphazard shotgun pattern of urbanization known as "sprawl."

Lot of record: A lot which is part of a recorded subdivision or a parcel of land which has been recorded, usually at a county recorder's office containing property tax records.

Mandatory referral: The process of referring specified proposals to the planning commission (and sometimes to other departments or agencies) for review. Such proposals might include rezoning requests or major capital improvements by another governmental agency. Under such requirements, often found in enabling legislation or a municipal charter, the planning commission must report whether the proposal conforms to its comprehensive plan or other policies. Increasingly, conventional mandatory referral procedures are becoming more rigorous through legislative or executive requirements for impact analysis.

Metes and bounds: A system of describing and identifying land by measures (metes) and direction (bounds) from an identifiable point of reference such as a monument or other marker, the corner of intersecting streets, or, in rural areas, a tree or other permanent feature. It is the most precise of the three most common forms of urban land description (the others are by street number of house and by blocks and lots in tract subdivision). It is used with precision where land values are high and, more loosely, in rural areas.

Mobile home (trailer): A factory-built home, equipped with all of the basic amenities of a conventional home (bath, kitchen, electricity), which can be moved to its site by attaching it whole or in sections to an automobile or truck. (A trailer is a much smaller mobile shelter, usually used for camping and outings rather than as a permanent dwelling.) Prefabricated modular units currently come complete with built-in furnishings, appliances, porches, and other extras. "Double-wides" and "triple-wides" are units connected together to form a single structure of size and roof design similar to that of a conventional home built on a foundation on site. Mobile home parks rent spaces with utility hookups to mobile home owners; sometimes they also rent the mobile homes. The parks range in size from a few parking spaces equipped with plumbing and electrical connections to elaborate mobile-home communities with swimming pools and community centers. About a quarter of the single-family home sales since 1968 have been captured by mobile homes.

Moratorium: In planning, a freeze on all new development pending the completion and adoption of a comprehensive plan. In recent years building moratoriums have also been instituted by water and sewer agencies when sewage treatment facilities are inadequate or when water shortages are threatened. They have also been voted into being by residents of communities whose schools and other public facilities have been overwhelmed by rapid growth. There are still a number of legal questions about such moratoriums to be resolved by the courts. Air basins already overburdened by air pollution may be next in line for building freezes.

Neighborhood: The smallest subarea in city planning, defined as a residential area whose residents have public facilities and social institutions in common, generally within walking distance of their homes. Informal face-to-face contacts and some communal consciousness, either through homeowners' associations or crisis alliances to ward off threatening developments and zone changes, also characterize a neighborhood.

24

Nonconforming use: A structure or use that is not permitted by its present district's zoning regulations. If it was established after the enactment of the ordinance, it is illegal and may be abated, but if it existed before the regulations, it is a legal nonconforming use and may continue, although a new or different nonconforming use may not replace it. Most ordinances provide that its extension or enlargement is not permissible. Many ordinances permit the restoration of the nonconforming premises when damaged by fire, earthquake, or some other catastrophe. Once the use is abandoned, however, there is no longer a right to its restoration and the future use of the premises must conform to the regulations. Some states provide for the cessation of such uses at the end of a prescribed amortization period equivalent to the life of the structure as an investment.

Nuisance: Anything that interferes with the use or enjoyment of property, endangers personal health or safety, or is offensive to the senses. There are many types of nuisances, and the law can be invoked to determine when, in fact, a nuisance exists and should be abated. Nuisance law forms part of the basis for zoning. The separation of uses through zoning, e.g., industrial from residential, helps to foster the enjoyment of residential areas from pollution, noise, congestion, and other characteristics of industrial areas. Performance standards, which are better able to measure degree of nuisance, have been developed as a way of dealing with activities by the way they perform, rather than as classes.

Official map: A detailed public-improvements plan adopted by the city council or county board of supervisors that protects the sites and rights-of-way shown on it from preemption by private development for a limited period, during which the required land can be acquired by conventional acquisition procedures. By reserving land for streets, parks, school sites, and public utilities, the community in turn is placed under an obligation to acquire these lands with reasonable promptness. This means that the specific properties to be purchased should be closely coordinated with the local capital improvement program and annual capital budgeting process.

Open land (OA) district: A zoning classification that limits the allowable uses to agriculture, recreation, parks, reservoirs, and water supply lands. OA districts are most commonly used for publicly owned lands of public agencies, but are also used in areas subject to flooding (flood plain zones) and other natural hazards. A variation of OA zoning is used in airport approach and clear zones where land beyond the landing runways must be kept free of obstructions and projections from the ground.

Open space: That part of the countryside which has not been developed and which is desirable for preservation in its natural state for ecological, historical, or recreational purposes, or in its cultivated state to preserve agricultural, forest, or urban greenbelt areas.

Parcel: A lot, or contiguous group of lots in single ownership or under single control, and usually considered a unit for purposes of development.

Peak hour: For any given highway, the sixty-minute period of the day during which it carries its highest volume of traffic. Usually this occurs during the morning or evening rush, when the majority of people attempts to get to or from work.

Performance standards: Zoning regulations providing specific criteria limiting the operations of certain industries, land uses, and buildings to acceptable levels of noise, air pollution emissions, odors, vibration, dust, dirt, glare, heat, fire hazards, wastes, traffic generation, and visual impact. This type of zoning may not bar an industry or use by specified type, but admits any use that can meet the particular standards of operation set for admission. Instead of classifying industries in districts under the headings "light," "heavy," or "unrestricted," it establishes measurable technical standards and classifies the industries in terms of their probable environmental impact. Terms such as "limited," "substantial," and "objectionable" determine the overall acceptability rating of a particular use.

Planned unit development (PUD): A self-contained development, often with a mixture of housing types and densities, in which the subdivision and zoning controls are applied to the project as a whole rather than to individual lots, as in most subdivisions. Therefore, densities are calculated for the entire development, usually permitting a trade-off between clustering of houses and provision of common open space.

Police power: The inherent right of a government to restrict an individual's conduct or use of property in order to protect the health, safety, welfare, and morals of the community. In the United States, this power must relate reasonably to these ends and must follow due processes of the law; but unlike the exercise of the state's power of eminent domain, no compensation need be paid for losses incurred as a result of police-power regulation.

Preliminary subdivision map: The first formal submission by a subdivider is usually in the form of a map with accompanying documents providing the information about the proposed subdivision required by the local subdivision ordinance. Generally the following information is contained in the preliminary map (see Figure 1): name of subdivision; its location, acreage, owner, and engineer or surveyor; the location of property lines, roads, existing utilities and their bearings and dimensions; names of adjoining properties; zoning classification of the property; proposed water, sewer, drainage, and public utility systems to be employed; names of new streets; lot numbers, setback lines, and lot dimensions; and the location of any easements, culverts, storm drains, creeks, ponds, or other significant natural features, including contours and adjacent structures. If the land is to be subdivided in sections, the preliminary map is often required to include a precise plan of streets, public facilities, and lots for the entire holding as well as the section being submitted for approval, so that the public agency can be assured at the outset that the pieces will fit together properly when the development is completed.

Principal use: The main use of land or structures as distinguished from a secondary or accessory use. A house is a principal use in a residential area; a garage or pool is an accessory use. Zoning ordinances will often establish a general rule that only one principal structure or use will be permitted on each lot. Drafters of such language generally have single-family areas in mind; but, unless application is clearly limited to such use, it can lead to unnecessary complications, such as requiring land to be subdivided in multifamily, commercial, or industrial districts where there is to be more than one principal structure or use on a lot or tract or requiring buildings to be joined merely to avoid the subdivision requirement.

27

OWNER & SUBDIVIDER
John R. McKinny
24 Valley Drive
Novato, California 94947
Telephone 881-4543

ENGINEER
Johnson and Harbeck Co.
135 Ferry Road
San Rafael, California

NOTES

1. Property is not presently being used.

2. Proposed use is single-family residential (8300 SF min).

3. Water will be supplied by city water district.

4. Fire protection will be supplied by city fire district.

5. Gas and electric will be supplied by P. G. & E.

6. Telephone will be supplied by telephone company.

7. Sewage disposal will be supplied by city sanitary district.

8. No public areas other than streets are proposed.

9. Total number of lots = 18.

10. Tentative map area = 6.83 acres.

11. Existing shrubs and trees on the property are to be removed as required for houses and streets, and trees will be planted in accordance with normal subdivision standards.

12. All buildings on site will be removed.

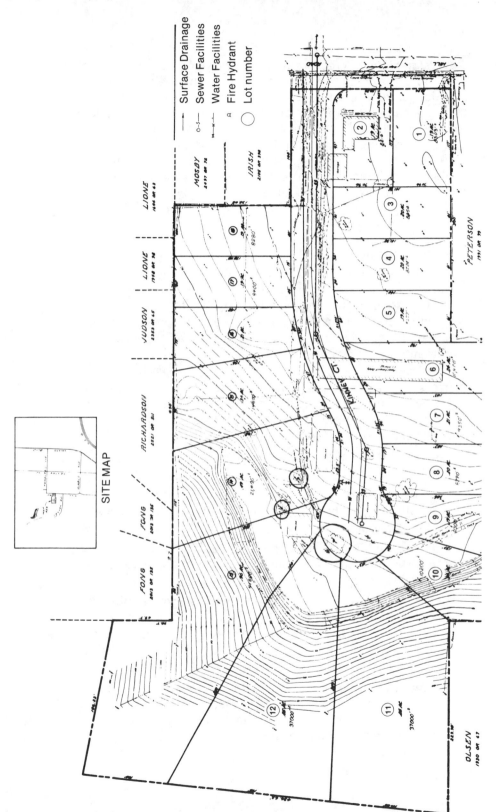

FIGURE 1. Example of information required on a preliminary subdivision map.

Reversion clause: A requirement that may accompany special use permit approval or a rezoning that returns the property to its prior zoning classification if a specified action, such as taking out a building permit or beginning construction, does not begin in a specified period of time, say, one year. This is a way of protecting a community against using permits or rezonings for speculative purposes. In the case of rezoning it is also illegal, since "automatic rezoning" does not follow required amendment procedures. This objection does not apply to expiration of special permits not involving a change in the zoning map or text.

Right-of-way: The right of passage over the property of another. The public may acquire it through implied dedication— accepted access over a period of time to a beach or lake shoreline, for example. More commonly, it refers to the land on which a road or railroad is located. The pathways over which utilities and drainage ways run are usually referred to as easements.

Road system: The classification of streets and highways by their diverse functions and design (see Figure 2). The following is the commonly used hierarchy of streets and highways for planning purposes:

Local street: A roadway allowing access to abutting land, serving local traffic only.

Collector: A street whose function is to channel traffic from local streets to major arterials; it has direct access to abutting properties.

Major arterial: A road that serves through-traffic movement across urban areas, often subject to controlled access from properties fronting on the right-of-way

Expressway: A divided multilane highway whose purpose is to move large volumes of through traffic from one part of a metropolitan area to another; intersections are separated by under- or overpasses at major intersections. It does not provide land-access service between intersections.

Freeway: A multilane highway with full grade separation, total control of access, median strips, and fencing, or landscaping strips along the sides. It basically serves intercity and interstate traffic.

Parkway: An expressway or freeway designed for non-commercial traffic only; usually located within a strip of landscaped park or natural vegetation.

Septic tank: A tank plus a leaching field or trenches in which the sewage is purified by bacterial action. It is distinct from a cesspool, which is merely a perforated buried tank that allows the liquid effluent to seep into the surrounding soils but retains most of the solids and must be periodically pumped out.

Setback regulations: The requirements of building laws that a building be set back a certain distance from the street or lot line either on the street level or at a prescribed height. Their aim is to allow more room for the pedestrian or reduce the obstruction to sunlight reaching the streets and lower stories of adjoining buildings.

Sewage system: A facility designed for the collection, removal, treatment, and disposal of waterborne sewage generated

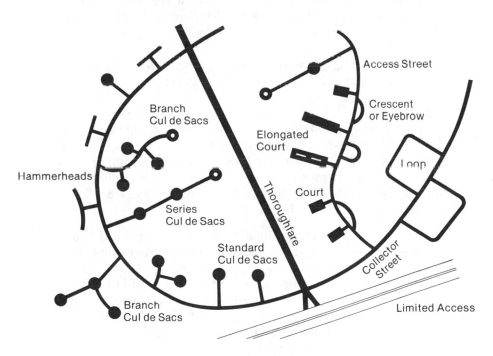

FIGURE 2. Road system designs.

within a given service area. It usually consists of a collection network of pipelines and a treatment facility to purify and discharge the treated wastes.

Site plan: A plan, to scale, showing uses and structures proposed for a parcel of land as required by the regulations involved. It includes lot lines, streets, building sites, reserved open space, buildings, major landscape features—both natural and manmade—and, depending on requirements, the locations of proposed utility lines.

Site plan review: The process whereby local officials, usually the planning commission and staff, review the site plans and maps of a developer to assure that they meet the stated purposes and standards of the zone, provide for the necessary public facilities such as roads and schools, and protect and preserve topographical features and adjacent properties through appropriate siting of structures and landscaping. It usually is required in connection with many flexible techniques. The process often allows considerable discretion to be exercised by local officials since it may deal with hard-to-define aesthetic and design considerations.

Special use; special use permit: The term "special use," with its numerous subclassifications, is so widely and variously used as to make useful definition difficult. In the simplest sense, from the administrator's point of view (and the applicant's) a use as of right is one where the permit can be issued on the basis of the application alone, and the applicant can proceed under the permit without further referrals, or reviews, other than normal inspections. Using the exclusion approach, a special use may then be defined as a use other than a use by (or as of) right.

Variations in this leftover group are numerous as to kind and as to procedures involved. Required special approvals may be by one or a combination of the following, among others: the governing body; the planning commission; the board of adjustment or hearing examiner; the architectural review board and/or other special-purpose review boards; and department heads or officials other than the zoning administrator, ranging through building, health, traffic and safety, and others.

Procedures progress from simple to extremely complex; from a meeting (or interchange of correspondence) between an applicant and an official required to check out a detail before the zoning administrator can issue a permit, to a series of complex presentations before boards and elected and appointed officials, involving public notice and hearings.

Spot zoning: The awarding of a use classification to an isolated parcel of land which is detrimental or incompatible with the uses of the surrounding area, particularly when such an act favors a particular owner. Such zoning has been held to be illegal by the courts on the grounds that it is unreasonable and capricious. A general plan or special circumstance such as historical value, environmental importance, or scenic value would justify special zoning for a small area.

Standards: While often used loosely to refer to all requirements in a zoning ordinance, the term usually is used to mean site design regulations such as lot area, height limits, frontage, landscaping, yards, and floor area ratio—as distinguished from use restrictions.

Strip zone: A melange of development, usually commercial, extending along both sides of a major street leading out of the center of a city. Usually a strip zone is a mixture of auto-oriented enterprises (e.g., gas stations, motels, and food stands), truck-dependent wholesaling, and light industrial enterprises, along with the once-rural homes and farms overtaken by the haphazard leapfrogging of unplanned sprawl. Strip development, with its incessant turning movements in and out of each enterprise's driveway, has so reduced the traffic-carrying capacity of major highways leading out of urban centers that the postwar limited-access freeway networks have become a necessity. In zoning terms, a strip zone may refer to a district consisting of a ribbon of highway commercial uses fronting both sides of a major arterial route.

Subdivision: The process of laying out a parcel of raw land into lots, blocks, streets, and public areas. Its purpose is the transformation of raw land into building sites. In most states, a subdivision is defined as the division of a tract of land into five or more lots. In many states the division of land into four lots or less is known as a lot split or land division, and in many jurisdictions it escapes the public improvement requirements of subdivision regulations. In rural and smaller towns, lot splits have been used as a loophole for land speculators to peddle lots without the front-end costs of improved streets, drains, and curbs usually required of subdividers subject to the subdivision ordinance.

Taking: The appropriation by government of private land for which compensation must be paid. Under the U.S. Constitution, property cannot be condemned through eminent domain for public use or public purpose without just compensation. This is reasonably clear when government buys land directly. But the "taking issue" is far less clear when the imposition of police-power controls diminishes the value of property considerably (as in inverse condemnation). A middle ground has been attempted to be struck through the enactment of compensable regulations which pay for the value lost.

Trip: The journey from the traveler's point of origin to the destination and the smallest unit of movement considered by transportation studies.

Trip generation: The dynamics that account for people making trips in autos or transit. Transportation studies generally try to balance the trip generation of households (by purpose, such as to go to work, shopping, or recreation) with the places that would attract them for these purposes. Generally the propensity of a person to journey to a place is based on the time-distance factor from origin to destination, modified by the attractiveness of the place—square footage in a shopping center and employment in an industrial area. The product of this exercise is a rough estimate of how a transportation system is being used and an approximation of what impact additional development or transportation facilities will have on the local transportation system.

Urban design: The attempt to give form, in terms of both beauty and function, to entire areas or to whole cities. The term implies a more fundamental approach than "beautification" and is concerned with the location, mass, and design of the various urban components. It combines the concerns of urban planning, architecture, and landscape architecture.

Urban fringe: An area at the edge of an urban area usually made up of mixed agricultural and urban land uses. Where leapfrogging or sprawl is the predominant pattern, this mixture of urban and rural may persist for several decades until the process of urbanization is completed.

Urban limit line (urban service area): An area, identified through official public policy, within which urban development will be allowed during a specified time period. Beyond this line, using a variety of growth management tools such as acreage zoning and limits on capital improvements, development is prohibited or strongly discouraged. The establishment of such service boundaries has become an important tool for implementing public decisions on where growth should occur and what kinds of services a community can afford to supply. Some communities have established several lines, intending them to correspond with the phasing of growth over an extended period of time.

Urban renewal: A governmental program generally aimed at the renovation of blighted urban areas through public expenditures for replacing slums with better housing, rehabilitating or conserving sound structures, and providing opportunities for new and better commercial, industrial, and public buildings as well as for an improved urban environment. Charles Abrams describes the history of the federal urban renewal program as follows:

Private enterprise was to be encouraged to serve as large a part of the need as possible [in the federal programs of the sixties] and slums and blighted areas were to be cleared and low-income families rehoused. To provide the sites, local public agencies (housing authorities or renewal agencies) were authorized by state laws to acquire the necessary land and buildings by eminent domain. The land was then written down from acquisition cost to reuse value with local government providing a third of the write-down loss and the federal government two-thirds . . . . The main weakness is that the program has assumed that rebuilding a few slum or blighted areas would automatically make a city sound. The city in the United States is at bay for reasons other than the slum problem. With middle- and upper-income families deserting it, with tax sources diminishing at the same time as the city becomes host to new waves of the nation's poor, a few reconstructed areas in or near its center cannot make it whole.[2]

Vacancy ratio: The ratio between the number of vacant units in a designated area and the total number of existing units within

[2] Abrams, *The Language of Cities.*

that area. Vacancy ratios, when used for planning, relocation, and other activities, can be misleading because they often do not sufficiently take into account such variables as (1) the actual condition of the unit or building, (2) the condition of public services or neighborhood quality relating to transit, safety, and other considerations, (3) the rent or purchase price levels of the available units, (4) the ability of prospective families and individuals to pay, and (5) special restrictions aimed at racial groups, children, and others.

Value, market: The price a willing buyer would presumably pay for a property when it is offered for sale by a willing seller in an open market. Estimates of market value are used in tax assessment procedures, eminent domain proceedings, and real estate appraisals.

Vested right: A right is vested when it has become absolute and fixed and cannot be defeated or denied by subsequent conditions or change in regulations, unless it is taken and paid for. There is no vested right to an existing zoning classification or to have zoning remain the same forever. However, once development has been started or has been completed, there is a right to maintain that particular use regardless of the classification given the property. In order for a nonconforming use to earn the right to continue when the zoning is changed, the right must have vested before the change. If the right to complete the development has not vested, it may not be built, no nonconforming use will be established, and the new regulations will have to be complied with.

Vested rights are often established by showing that some development permit has been obtained and substantial construction on the project started. How much construction or land improvements must have been completed before the rights are vested varies among the states. In some states application for a building permit or other development approval may be sufficient to establish a vested right to complete a project. Others may require substantial investment and beginning of construction on the land, with completion of structures that are unique to the planned project.

Windfalls and wipeouts: The conferring of great financial benefits ("windfalls") or losses ("wipeouts") on a property owner as a result of public action. Zoning, for example, can create very high land values in areas zoned for high-density development, or it can severely reduce value by zoning for low-density or extensive uses, as in the enactment of restrictive environmental controls. Similarly, a highway or sewer extension decision can have a great effect on land values, as can a variety of other public regulatory or capital investment decisions. Recognizing the possible injustices created by these actions, many remedies have been considered in an effort to "recapture" windfall profits by the public, to avoid wipeouts, and to trade windfalls for wipeouts. It has been done in some other English-speaking countries; at present, however, the work in this area remains theoretical and conceptual, although it has generated considerable interest and a growing literature.

Yard: The unbuilt-upon space on a building lot situated between the front, rear, or side wall of a building and the nearest lot line. It is more common in planning and zoning to be more specific and designate the front yard, side yard, and rear or back yard as the spaces between those respective sides of the building and the adjoining lot line.

Zoning: "Zoning is a police power measure, enacted by units of local government under permissive state legislation. Zoning regulations establish, in advance of applications for development, groups of permitted uses that vary from district to district."[3] They also control the placement, height, bulk, and coverage of structures within each of the districts into which the jurisdiction is divided by the zoning map, which is a part of the zoning ordinance.

Zoning district: A section of a city or county designated in the zoning ordinance text and (usually) delineated on the zoning map, in which requirements for the use of land and building and development standards are prescribed. Within each district, all requirements must be uniform. A jurisdiction may have as few as two or three or as many as fifty districts, depending on circumstances and needs.

[3] John Reps, "Requiem for Zoning," in *Taming Megalopolis* (New York: Anchor Books, 1967).

A Layperson's Guide to the Planning Process and the Tools That Make It Work

3

Athens expects every citizen to take an interest in public affairs. We do believe in knowledge as a guide to action: we have the power of thinking before we act and of acting too. I would have you fix your eyes upon Athens day by day, contemplate her potentiality, not merely what she is, but what she has the power to be. Reflect that her glory has been built up by men who know their duty and had the courage to do it. Make them your examples and learn from them.

—Pericles

The role of the planning commissioner in the planning process is very often not well understood by the elected officials who appoint commissioners, the staff planners, or the commissioners themselves. For several years this writer collected responses to a questionnaire (see Appendix G) given at several national conferences and workshops for planning commissioners around the nation.[1] The thrust of this questionnaire was to find out what professional planners felt was the ideal planning commission operation and what the responding commissioners were actually encountering in their jobs. (In all there were over 500 usable responses.)

The significant findings of this survey were as follows:

a. **Tools with which to work:** While 61 percent of the respondents said that their agency had an up-to-date general

[1] The questionnaire and its results are reproduced for illustrative purposes only. The reader is cautioned against concluding that the results of the survey are in any way conclusive, fully representative, or statistically reliable as a national picture, but they do show the major problems and shortcomings in quite a few places.

plan (revised and adopted within the past three years) and 86 percent stated that their agency had general plan documents and maps readily available to the public, over two-fifths (41 percent) did not have a general plan with action programs to implement the goals and policies of the plan. Over a third (35 percent) did not have an up-to-date map of existing land use to work with, and 31 percent did not have a professionally trained planning staff that keeps up to date through continuing education and retraining.

b. **Preparation for the job:** Although 77 percent of the respondents had read a book on planning or cities, their job preparation was often woefully minimal. For example, 39 percent had never had a study session with their staff to go over procedures and matters of commissioner-staff relationships as distinguised from matters associated with agenda items. Slightly more (40 percent) had never had a meeting with their city or county attorney to learn their legal powers, limitations, and other information. However, 72 percent had been given a "lesson" by their staff on the importance of collecting findings before making decisions and how to do so. An even higher number (85 percent) had talked or agreed among their colleagues about the procedures to be followed.

c. **Integration with agency functions and external contracts:** The survey indicated that commissioners tended to work in isolation from other planning activities. Almost three-fifths (59 percent) had never even seen a work program for their agency. Two-thirds (67 percent) had never participated in hiring a consultant, while 40 percent had never been asked to review the budget for the planning department or participate in developing a work program for their agency. About a third (34 percent) had never met as a commission with their own city council or county board of supervisors. Meetings with neighboring planning commissions were even less common, with 40 percent never having participated in one. A full two-thirds (67 percent) had never held a public forum to ask citizens what they want of the commission and planning program for their community.

d. **Intimidation and dependency:** A surprising number of commissioners (42 percent) confessed to having voted yes on a zone change or other such proposal when they really wanted to vote no. An equal percentage had been intimidated by an applicant, but only 5 percent had ever been intimidated by their staff or felt at their mercy. However, 30 percent felt they were at the point where they had become almost totally dependent on their staff for ideas and the bases for making decisions. The one bright spot was that a full 60 percent had had the courage at one time or another to say, "We don't know and are not ready to make a decision . . . let's think awhile and make no decision until we know what we are doing." An even larger number (65 percent) had been able to tell their staff what they wanted when the staff disappointed them or failed to present something the way the commissioners wanted it presented.

e. **Attitudes:** Despite the handicaps reported in the question-naire as a whole, only 27 percent of the respondents felt that their planning commission was impotent or of no value. However, 39 percent felt that decisions were sometimes made almost entirely on the basis of the proponent or opponent (best debator wins).

The salient thing that emerged from this survey is that to a very unhealthy extent, planning commissioners are isolated from everyone else involved in the local planning process. It must be remembered that this sampling was drawn from the relatively affluent, sophisticated, and reasonably experienced commissioners who attend national conferences. The same survey taken at local workshops in Oregon and California where the respondents are from poorer, more rural communities and are less experienced on the job showed higher degrees of isolation, dependency on staff, and lack of proper tools with which to work. These surveys strongly suggest that the best way to improve the performance of planning commissions is not better techniques and planning methodology but rather stronger interaction with all the other people involved in the planning process.

The city of Berkeley, California, which has one of the most sophisticated and extensive citizen participation systems in the nation, surveyed all of its boards and commissions in the fall of 1980.[2] The responses of both commissioners (25 percent) and their staff (40 percent) highlight some of the problems of citizens who work in local government.

Almost half (47 percent) of the commissioners believed that

[2] Barry Rosen, *Citizens in Government: The Effectiveness of Berkeley's Boards and Commissions.* (Berkeley: City manager's office, 1981).

their group lacked enough information to make good decisions. Although 71 percent felt that they received enough staff support to carry out the functions of their group effectively, 45 percent of the staff respondents felt they did not have enough time to give to their commission duties. On the matter of coordination with the city council, 44 percent of the commissioners would have appreciated additional input from the council during the process of developing reports, while only 30 percent of the staff felt that they needed to establish better working relationships with the council in order to function more effectively. The major suggestions made by commissioners included a general orientation process for all new commissioners (71 percent) and better procedures for filling commission vacancies (68 percent). Staff members suggested overwhelmingly (90 percent) that regular meetings between commission chairpersons and staff liaisons be established to plan activities and agenda items. See the following list for basic ideas on improving a commission's role in the planning process.

Fourteen Ways to Build a Better Commission

1. Develop and adopt bylaws and procedures, and stick to them.
2. Develop and make available to anyone who wants them good and reliable information, data, and maps.
3. Prepare and maintain an adequate general plan, refer to it, and make decisions that are consistent with its policies and also implement them.
4. Annually reexamine what you are doing as a commission, how well you are doing it, and how to do it better.
5. Outline a year's work on *active* planning and stick to it. Don't confuse development permit processing (reactive planning or plan review) with *real* planning.
6. Ask to participate in preparing the planning agency's budget.
7. Meet periodically with your city council or county board to exchange ideas and to assess your mutual objectives.
8. Consider a public forum every year or so. Ask people (your "clients") how things are going and what they want done (if anything).
9. Tell your staff what you want, how you want material presented to you, etc. Don't be a passive commission that waits for "the experts" to tell you what to do next.

10. Attend some short courses on new planning techniques or the latest in land-use law, and expect your staff to do the same.

11. Tour about as a commission to see what others are doing. Sometimes you will be uplifted to find out how many light years ahead of your neighbors you really are, and sometimes you'll get some ideas worth borrowing.

12. Appoint a commission representative to appear before the elected body when it is necessary to explain or sell an action. Don't expect staff to do your job.

13. Lobby for good planning. If you don't, who will?

14. Take time to orient new commissioners to the job. (Remember how tough it was to get the hang of it when *you* were a new member of your commission.)

One of the underlying causes of commissioners' difficulties in doing effective planning has been what Franklyn Beal described as the "traditional approach to planning," which reigned supreme in the era between World War II and the mid-seventies. While it's being supplanted in good planning schools and agencies, many planners who swallowed the traditional approach in their formative years as students and professionals are now directors of agencies, and what follows may well be all they ever learned.

The essence of our traditional approach to planning has been to view the city as a large design project. The community is thought to have a spacial plastic form that can be grasped and reduced to manipulation and presentation by graphic means. Planning, according to this view, is the process of forming a picture of a future physical pattern and developing the control measures that are needed to move the community toward the goal. The objective is to make the community look like the map of the future and the goals, sometimes stated but often only implicit in the map, are convenience, order, efficiency, economy, and beauty.

Typically, the city planning effort begins with an extensive survey of existing conditions and predictions of the number of people, cars, jobs, etc., that could be expected in the next 20 years. Studies are made of the existing land use, the population, the economy, the housing stock, the circulation system, and the community utilities and facilities. The studies are, for the most part, quantitative descriptions and predictions, but to a lesser extent, they deal with the qualitative features of the system. Once the studies and projections are completed, the estimates of people, vehicles, households, and employment are converted into the common denominator — acres of land needed to accommodate each use. The conversion from people (or jobs or whatever) to land is based upon existing ratios and modified by national averages and standards promulgated by specialists in various fields (e.g., five acres of playground space for each neighborhood of 1,000 families). The final task is to distribute these future land requirements, to establish the proper design that will accommodate the anticipated growth. The criteria used to determine appropriate locations for each category of use are based upon the existing pattern, intuition ("don't put noisy factories next to single family homes"), and the judgment of specialists (the radius of the service area for a neighborhood recreation center should be no greater than one-quarter mile).

Once the picture of the future is complete, it is accepted by the planning commission as the city plan.[3]

H. Wentworth Eldridge of the Harvard faculty in urban planning summarized the traditional planning process more succinctly as a six-stage progression.

1. setting values or goals

2. toting up available resources

3. making alternate possible plans

4. selecting "the" plan

5. administering the plan

6. finally Utopia![4]

Fred Bair, former executive director of the Florida Planning and Zoning Association, defined this kind of planning process

[3] Franklyn Beal, "Defining Development Objectives," in *Principles and Practice of Urban Planning* (Chicago: International City Managers Association, 1968). Used by permission.

[4] H. Wentworth Eldridge, *World Capitals* (Garden City, N.Y.: Anchor Press-Doubleday, 1975).

with a dangling preposition: "Planning is whatever there are federal grants in aid of." To this must be added the fact that planning has been whatever the state laws and courts consider adequate.[5]

To really work, however, a general plan should be excellent. The following list contains ten criteria that a worthwhile general plan should meet.

1. **It shows how the community can keep and improve its livability in the face of change.** The definition of livability lies in the minds of the residents, something it would be well for planners to check out first, so they'll know what the plan is for in terms of what people value. In Portland, Oregon, a 1981 survey of city residents' subjective ideas of what livability was in what EPA classed as one of the United States' most livable cities found:[6]

   a. *In their mental images the mountains, hills, rivers, and greenery predominated over manmade features such as parks, bridges, and districts. Even the rain and climate were dominant over the built-up areas.*

   b. *Most important of all was the social environment. In this regard most of the respondents referred to the positive*

---

[5] In one case I worked on, the issue focused on whether or not the city's general plan was adequate enough to guide the approval stage of a gigantic development. The judge's decision in this case (*City of Oakland* v. *City of Alameda*) stated very clearly that a city has a legal responsibility to keep its general plan in working order:

Without question the evidence [is] clear that for a general plan to be viable and useful it needs to be changed. . . . The mere passage of time is such that it requires review. From the evidence there has been no review since the plan's initial adoption. The fact that a developer . . . actually has plans that are "very good" is still not enough to overcome the inadequacies of a general plan. The fact that one might say with hindsight the actual proposed development plans are good does not cure defects which exist in the general plan and its elements.

It is essential that the general plan consider all factors; consideration is the key, not a projection of a court of what results might have resulted from such consideration. . . .

Inasmuch as the court has hereinabove determined that the City of Alameda's General Plan is invalid, any finding that the planned development implements the general plan is a nullity.

[6] Excerpted from Tom Gihring, "Portland's Self Image and the Incomprehensible Plan," *Newsletter, A.P.A.* (Oregon Chapter), vol. 17, no. 1, January–February 1981.

qualities of other residents, their cultural and economic activities, and the availability of public services. For some this might mean small-town atmosphere, relatively low densities so that continued auto use is still easy and most destinations are accessible and convenient.

    c. The park system was considered very important in reinforcing the city's "affinity to nature" — an aspect of the country in the city which again was an expression of the preference for a small-town atmosphere at least equal to the value of the system for recreation and leisure activities.

2. **It should provide clear guidance for day-to-day decisions including how any single piece of development fits in with the rest.** This means that urbanizable land should be clearly identified and separated from rural land and open space. It should be precise enough so that plans for sewage collection and treatment, water supply, police and fire service levels, and new school enrollments can be confidently and accurately derived from the plan. Unfortunately, this will take the fun out of planning for those who are used to drawing broad meandering "planning area" lines, usually painted gray. At public hearings, it was easy to evade questions from property owners about whether they were inside or out by saying "This line has no definite location — it's for planning purposes only"!

3. **An excellent plan should give everyone a good focus on solving some present problems.** In one western city, the plan consisted of a status quo map of the built-up areas and a series of "growth management lines" showing how far utilities would be extended beyond "the fringe" in five-year increments. At one public hearing, a grizzled old apple farmer demolished the city team's smugness by observing: "How am I supposed to believe everything's going to be hunky-dory in the areas you annex beyond those lines, when everything now inside them is planned to continue to go to hell in a handbasket?"

4. **It shows how to get from here to there.** Each proposal in the plan should be backed up with the measures which will make it happen. These measures, especially the ones that require money, should be substantiated by factual knowledge of the real world. Thus, a plan proposal to involve the local school district in expanding playgrounds won't touch base with reality if, for the foreseeable future, the district will be closing many of its schools and paring its budget in the face of declining enrollments and available funds. A more realistic and

45

workable plan would deal with the problem of school site and building recycling.

5. **It should deal with important visual concerns in a three-dimensional way.** For example, in one city the plan was overhauled to allow add-a-rentals, row housing, and mobile homes in formerly pure single-family districts. People were naturally apprehensive about what they had not experienced, or even worse, some stereotype. Eye-level illustrations of precisely what was being proposed and how it would benignly fit with what existed were badly needed. Instead, the people got disconnected, fuzzy policy statements like "X city needs to attain its housing goals by diversification within the existing neighborhood framework," and assurances that every departure from the status quo would require at least one public hearing and two levels of review.

6. **It should deal with how things will work as well as where they will go.** Nowhere has the validity of this principle been more clearly demonstrated than in the literally thousands of mismatches between highways and land use. The scenario often played out in as little as a decade goes like this:

Stage I.   Ricky Tick Road connects Sapsucker City with Babbittville, passing through the pleasant farmland of Pettipoint County.

Stage II. Babbittville has zoned its part of the road as solid strip commercial, and soon it takes longer and longer to get through the congestion and on to Sapsucker City.

Stage III. Meanwhile Sapsucker's downtown is dying because the county has allowed a giant shopping center–industrial park–mobile home retirement village to be built just beyond the city limits with lots of free parking, but there is no improvement in the two-lane width of Ricky Tick Road, so traffic jams in peak hours and weekends are miles long.

Stage IV. Everyone agrees that traffic is a mess. The state draws up a plan for a freeway with cloverleaf exits to the centers of Babbittville, Sapsucker City, and lots of places in between.

Stage V.   The freeway eats out the heart of both cities, and explosive growth takes place in the new commuter corridor. Within three to five years, the journey between the two places takes longer on the new

46

freeway than it does on old Ricky Tick Road, because every interchange along the freeway route was zoned shopping center commercial or "planned" industrial and is intensively developed because of "easy access."

Stage VI. The freeway, commonly known as "blood alley" because of the hazardous conditions created at the ramps, which discharge into narrow old farm roads, is restudied for potential conversion to a $4-billion elevated light rail corridor known as ABORT (Alternative Babbittville Overhead Rapid Transit).

7. **The plan should have a strategy for positive change for older built-up areas.** While Europe has enchanted tourists with city areas hundreds of years old, the older urban areas of the United States have become blighted and in many cases nearly abandoned. One magazine predicts that these inner-city problems will be exported to the suburbs in the eighties:

There in the urban fringes they will be both less visible and harder to solve. . . . Given the nationwide scarcity and the inflated costs of inner-city rentals, where do the lower-income people go? More and more, they go to the older housing, now wearing out, that the Veterans Administration and the Federal Housing Administration financed in the post–World War II years. . . . In the South and West where population is shifting but housing remains tight, pushouts are also moving to fringe trailer courts and quickie prefab tracts, which often develop the characteristics of slums. [7]

So far very few plans have begun to shift away from urban renewal and gentrification programs to proposals that deal with problems of pushouts (e.g., condominium conversion ordinances protecting low- and moderate-income tenants).

8. **The plan should have a timing strategy that does such things as balance supply with demand for services and new facilities.** An excellent plan will pace as well as place new development.

9. **It should capture local policy in a way that is clear and comprehensible to the average citizen, so that in the future average citizens can defend the plan effectively**

[7] "Gentrified Cities, Suburbanized Slums," in *Next,* vol. 2, no. 2, March/April 1981.

and intelligently. The goals and policies in a plan should be explicit enough to allow the "making of findings" by future commissions reviewing development proposals.

10. **The plan should be clearly understood to be an obligation and commitment on the part of both the elected officials and commissioners who adopt the plan and those who succeed them.** This requires the combing out of weasel words and phrases such as "critical environmental features shall be preserved *where feasible*," or "affordable housing shall be provided for all residents as the opportunities to do so arise."

It also requires that the plan point in a single direction, rather than being a compendium of incompatible alternatives. If the direction originally chosen needs adjustment, then the changes should be made in public with due process, rather than picking a different page of the plan to justify a shift from previous decisions.

This is a good place to stop reading and check out your community's general plan against these simple criteria.

Perhaps the most important role the planning commission can play in improving the planning process is in helping develop and then working from a sharply defined set of goals and objectives. Many professional planners now believe that useful technical planning can *only* occur when there is first a clear set of statements about what the planning is *for*. Professional planners have usually not had the advantage of these prerequisites, but either have borrowed goals that were currently acceptable because they are embedded in someone else's plan or have made up vague "motherhood and flag" abstractions such as "the plan seeks a strong and vital commercial center" or "the city should plan for ample open space, residential balance, and a better living environment." No one can argue with goals like these, but neither can anyone translate them into actions to attain these ends.

The planning commission and the other citizens participating in the planning process should not accept the packaged rhetoric with which staff or consultants often preface their technical reports. Rather, they should take the lead in directing their planners to develop guidelines from which the planning process can operate. These guidelines, sometimes called a policy plan, should be based on two main sources. First, many

48

of the policies already exist, and the local government agencies and departments have been following them for some time. The commission and citizens' study committees should bring these operating policies together and assess them against this second source of policy goals, these being the ones the commission and committees set up as their own desired direction for the community's future.

For example, the commission may decide that the rate of future growth should be closely controlled to prevent further leapfrogging and sprawl. This would mean that sewer and water extensions, which are major growth-inducing factors, should be used instead to shape future urban growth toward compactness around existing development. However, a check of the utilities' operational policies may reveal that decisions for extensions do not consider the impact they have on future development. The managers of the utilities may consider them an inexhaustible service to be extended to anyone who can raise the cash to pay for it. A change of view on the part of the management may, therefore, be one of the objectives of the plan implementation program. In one instance, the notion of "we're not going to get mixed up in land-use planning, we're simply meeting the needs of our customers" could not be dislodged, so it was necessary to dislodge the directors of the utility district in the next election. This, too, can be a legitimate action for implementing a policy plan.

There are four levels to a policy statement. Using as an example a partial set of community goals from a suburban California city of 35,000 developed by five neighborhood committees and the planning commission, we have the following:[8]

I. **Goal:** Preserve the small-town rural character [of the city] even if it means forsaking some personal conveniences and new technologies.

II. **Objective:** To sustain the quality [of the city] and the rural character, provide for slow and orderly growth . . . to reach a maximum population (in the city's planning area) of 70,000 to 80,000 over the next thirty years.

[8] An older, more urban community would have goals and objectives with a different emphasis than these, e.g., providing a climate to attract new commercial growth, rather than controlling and limiting such development.

Objective: Open space and hill ridge lines must be protected and new growth must be in harmony with its natural setting.

Objective: Increase the "place to work function," but primarily in order to reduce out-commuting of residents, rather than to bring new people into the community. Likewise, any expansion of the "place to shop function" is to be for the benefit of residents rather than as a magnet for out-of-area shoppers. In short, the committees do not see the city as competing with nearby cities having regional shopping centers or for major or intensive urban facilities.

III. **Targets** for protection of open space and hill ridge lines. Natural features to be preserved:

1. The wooded backdrop of major hills that forms the skyline of the valley in which the city is located.

2. The San Francisco Bay frontage and its adjoining marshlands.

3. Creeks and low, marshy drainage areas and their related tree and plant formation (e.g., floodplains).

4. Knolls, ridgetops, and rolling grassy land forms.

5. The river and its adjoining marshlands.

6. Rock outcroppings.

7. Tree and shrub masses, grass, wildflowers, and topsoil.

Target: Future housing policy to preserve small-town rural character.

1. Future housing should integrate single-family units with the various multifamily units, emphasizing single-family units in the balance, and should take place on larger lot sizes; emphasize clustering techniques; and include "community centers."

2. Stress single-family units in the housing mix by restricting multifamily units to 10 percent of all new housing starts with one-half of the 10 percent being apartments.

3. Preserve and maintain the existing stock of housing in the city.

IV. **Implementation** guidelines (worked out with staff)

A. Recommendations specific to hillsides:

1. Prohibit any development on slopes in excess of 35 percent and 300 feet above sea level.

2. Restrict cutting, filling, and grading on the hillsides except to provide access or in cases where grading complements natural landforms.

3. Development in the hillsides should complement the natural environment by using indigenous planting and earth-color exteriors [for structures].

B. Shopping recommendations:

1. The regional shopping center envisioned in the 1970 downtown plan should be scaled down to fit a market consistent with the city area population limit.

2. Do not permit the development of a regional shopping center or major department store.

C. Density growth controls:

1. The growth rate of the city should be restricted to 2 percent per year.

2. The land designated as open space in the countywide plan should be excluded from development.

3. The average density on the remaining land should be 2.4 units/acre on flat land, with density on sloping land reached by doubling the density allowed by the present general plan slope policy.[9]

---

[9] For those whose inclinations run to officially approved ways of addressing issues in a general plan, the State of California's definitions developed to make references to these terms in state laws clearer are presented. The terms are ranked from the most general to the most specific. From the Office of Planning and Research, *General Plan Guidelines* (Sacramento: State of California, 1980).

Policy (1): A collective term describing those parts of a general plan that guide action, including goals, objectives, policies, principles, plan proposals, and standards in both the text and diagrams.

Goal: The ultimate purpose of an effort stated in a way that is general in nature and immeasurable. *Example:* "To enhance the open-space amenities of the community."

Objective: A measurable goal. *Example:* "To reduce peak-hour traffic congestion to service level 'C' by 1984."

Policy (2): A specific statement guiding action and implying clear commitment. *Example:* "Recreational uses in wildlife refuges and nature preserves shall be limited to those activities which are compatible with maintaining the environment with a minimum of disruption, such as hiking or horseback riding."

Principle: An assumption guiding plan proposals, standards, and implementation. *Example:* "A neighborhood is bounded by arterial streets which carry through-traffic and which are located so as to avoid unnecessary traffic within the neighborhood."

Plan proposal: An explanation of how policies specifically apply to an area. *Example:* "Establish a greenbelt along River X running from point Y to point Z." *Note:* A plan proposal can also take the form of a diagram.

Any plan worth doing must have specific means to the ends that will be adopted. There are many tools for guiding growth and change, and the list grows longer with each new technique created by planners and upheld by the courts. A partial list of these tools is given here:

A. **Zoning:** One of the local jurisdiction's basic powers is to regulate land use, and this is the oldest power in use. Many commissions have trouble with the apparent conflict between zoning powers and property rights, especially when property is to be downzoned to a less intensive use. However, when there is a reasonable public purpose for the change and the property is not being singled out for discriminatory treatment, then the change is probably legal. Thus, it is illegal to force a property owner to leave land vacant in order to provide the public with the amenity of open space, but the land use may be restricted to avoid imposing a cost on others. Zoning power ranges from requiring height and setback requirements where buildings would be detrimental to the development and enjoyment of other properties all the way to flood-plain zoning, where development is almost totally restricted in order to keep such development from creating additional flooding problems elsewhere as well as putting lives and buildings in harm's way. Such flood-plain zoning zones the flatlands next to waterways for farming, recreation, and wildlife and aquatic habitat. "Inverse condemnation" and all the other names for illegal "takings" occur when zoning is used in place of eminent domain to compel a private property owner to undertake an activity to benefit the public at his or her expense.

B. **Open-space protection and acquisition:** Most of the recently urbanized lands in the metropolitan regions of America seem to fit Ian McHarg's definition of "low-grade urban tissue" which is "neither city nor country, neither

---

Standard: A specific, often quantified guideline defining the relationship between two or more variables. Standards can often directly translate into regulatory controls. *Example:* Three to six dwelling units per net acre (low-density residential).

Implementation program (action program): A coordinated set of measures to carry out the policies of the general plan. *Example:* Open-space action program for implementing open-space policies.

Implementation measure: An action, procedure, program, or technique that carries out general plan policy. *Example:* "Develop a geologic hazard overlay zoning classification and apply it to all geologic hazard areas identified in the general plan."

convenient nor beautiful, neither grand nor humane, neither civilized nor rural, nor wild."

In far too many places, open spaces are really the vacant, leftover, and useless remnants of the urbanization process. Neither properly located nor grouped together in sufficient size to provide habitats for animals, recreation for people, or even feasible food-growing space, they represent a major reason for the new discontent. The Rockefeller task force report on land use and growth, *The Use of Land: A Citizen's Policy Guide to Urban Growth,* lists four kinds of land that it makes eminent good sense to keep in a natural state or at least protected from development. They include:

1. **Areas of critical environmental concern,** areas with important cultural or natural characteristics that development would interfere with. Types of land include: coastal and inland wetlands; flood plains of rivers, lakes, and streams; areas of unstable soils and high seismic activity; steep slopes and ridge tops; rare or valuable ecosystems, valuable forests, and related lands; and historic districts.

2. **Areas required for future public recreation.**

3. **Areas that would serve as buffer zones between urban areas** and would have a strategic significance in controlling the pattern of future development.

4. **Unique and highly productive farmland** which might also promote the buffer zone function.

Types 2 and 3 will probably continue to be the responsibility of local, county, and regional governments. An open-space program should identify the areas to be left free of development and enact the appropriate ordinances to implement the plan.

Some methods of acquiring open space are listed here:

1. **Purchase by condemnation:** Because public funds are usually in short supply for buying open-space land, only the properties having the highest priorities in accordance with an open-space and conservation plan should be bought outright.

2. **Donations** are often feasible for owners looking for tax advantages or a way to perpetuate their names in the community.

3. **Purchase of easements and less than full development rights** is often advisable when heavy public use of the

property is not contemplated. For example, the purchase of the residential development rights of a farm that the county wishes to keep in agriculture as part of a greenbelt should cost considerably less than buying full title to the property. Purchase of easements allowing public fishing, hiking, or horseback riding rights on a piece of privately owned land is another form of this kind of acquisition of open space.

4. **Sale-leasebacks** allow a public agency to acquire title to lands, then rent them out to private tenants for open-space uses. Thus the owner of the hypothetical farm might realize some cash from the sale but be able to keep the land in food production without property tax burdens.

5. **Contracts:** Some areas, such as California, preserve agricultural open space by offering farmers and ranchers agricultural preserve contracts whereby in return for keeping the land in agriculture rather than converting to other uses, the owner receives a tax break in the form of a tax assessment based on the agricultural value of the land rather than full market value.

6. **Regulation:** More and more jurisdictions are acquiring open space by use of special provisions of their zoning and subdivision ordinances. In zoning, open space is preserved by low-density controls (e.g., one unit per sixty acres) or acquired by allowing higher residential densities or smaller lot sizes in return for open space. In subdivisions, open space is gained through clustering of lots (see discussion on PUDs), or by simply requiring either an outright dedication of a certain fixed percent of the land to be subdivided or a cash payment in lieu of dedication.

7. **Tax deferral:** In some states, it may be possible to defer taxes on open-space lands as long as they remain in a use considered to be an open-space use, e.g., timber growth areas in Virginia.

C. **Managed growth:** Ideally a managed growth plan would balance expected increases in population with revenue flows and new costs for services and capital outlays. Most managed growth schemes tend to drive the cost of new housing up by holding a lid on supply while demand soars. Many of them have "an affordable housing provision" whereby projects selected for approval must include a percentage of units priced for occupancy by low- and moderate-income families, so that the exclusionary aspects of staged growth programs may be avoided.

In setting limits to growth, politics has seemed to govern more than laws have, because almost all states allow local governments to control the density of land use and the extension of public utilities. Thus far the managed growth strategies fall into the following categories:

1. **Undeclared moratorium:** The usual tactic here is to zone the land into very low-density zones, allowing the local governments to remove the restrictions (change the zone) as they approve developments they like and refuse those they don't. This makes the slowdown of growth unchallengable unless there is a strict state requirement about zoning conforming to a general plan. However, in such cases, zone changing becomes a two-step process: first, amend the plan; then change the zone to conform and approve the development.

2. **Interim zoning:** This occurs when a jurisdiction wishes to have a breathing spell in order to plan for an area's growth. The area is usually downzoned as a study zone with all requests for development handled as conditional use permits until the plan is prepared.

3. **Environmental moratorium:** This occurs when there is a lack of treatment capacity in the sewage plant, a threatened water shortage, or threatened damage to environmental values such as would be posed by dredging or filling a marshy area. A ban on sewer and water hookups may be imposed to protect water quality or avoid causing current users to suffer from an insufficient water supply.

   However, it has been argued that it may be unjust to place the consequences of past official neglect of the need for adequate sewage treatment and water supply capacities on the producers of housing. This is a gray area in the courts. Generally they have found that utilities not only have an obligation to serve the existing population but should also anticipate the future growth of their service area—but only when the demand can be met by existing supplies or capacities (e.g., *Crocker* v. *Spring Valley Water Company* decision of the California Supreme Court).

4. **Population capacity laws:** Places like Petaluma, California, and Boca Raton, Florida, voted for laws that set maximum population limits on the cities or limit residential building permits to a specified annual quota. In the case of Petaluma, a lower court found that a numerical limit on growth violated the general population's "constitutional right to travel and settle." This constitutional question of local sovereignty on growth

control versus "the right to travel" was not settled by the Appeals Court; the ruling overturning the lower court was based on the issue of standing. The Supreme Court declined to review the case, thus permitting the ordinance to stand.

On the other hand, when Fairfax County, Virginia, required developers of residential projects with fifty units or more to allocate 15 percent of the units to low- and moderate-income families, the Virginia courts struck the requirement down as "socioeconomic" zoning, claiming that requiring home sales at prices below the market is a taking for public purposes. (This finding was made despite the fact that the developer received compensating density bonuses for providing such housing.)

5. **Development timing:** So far the prime example of this kind of growth control has been created in the town of Ramapo, New York. Here, the town has deferred development rights for large areas of the township for up to 18 years, largely by staying the extension of public utilities. Timing ordinances should have a meaningful schedule for development timing and a capital improvement commitment to back it up. There should also be tax reductions for properties whose development rights have been postponed in this way. There should be provision for low- and moderate-income housing in order to make the ordinance nonexclusionary.

Finally, any local community needs to have its plans address the regional implications of local growth policies. For example, a small suburb like Ramapo is probably only a tiny part of the regional housing market, so the net effect of its slow-growth regulations may be to divert housing demand to other nearby places that have not yet "protected" themselves by pulling up their own local drawbridges.

As the judge in the *City of Oakland* v. *City of Alameda* case pointed out, over time a general plan can degenerate into "a nullity" if it remains unchanged. Therefore, it is essential to pay attention to the planning part of a commission's duties with at least one meeting per month for advance planning and review of what's happening in the community. For example, one very useful exercise is a field trip to see how projects that were recently approved look when they're actually built. Such inspections will reveal whether things actually came out the way everyone thought they would, or whether there are glaring loopholes in the development review or planning process. Periodic meetings with board of adjustment and hearing's officers should be held to identify recurring problems that may be symptoms of zoning ordinance inadequacies.

Study meetings should be closed to all the bits of property and project business that use up the time at regular meetings. In addition to maintaining and amending a general plan and its elements, advance planning meetings could cover the following:

a. Capital improvement programs

b. Review of the status of the general plan and progress in its application

c. Consultation with public officials and agencies; utility companies; civic, educational, and other organizations; plus citizens, with relation to carrying out the general plan

d. Review and report to elected officials on the conformity with the general plan of proposed public works, acquisitions, disposals, or abandonments of property for each fiscal year covered by the plan

e. Preparation and maintenance of area, community, or neighborhood plans, and action on amendments to them

If your commission is not carrying out any of these duties, then the planning process is being seriously neglected. The commission is really a zoning board, and the general plan of your community may be well on the way to being as suspect as Alameda's.

Prerequisites to Doing
an Effective Job

4

Ineffective commissioners *are* nowhere men (and women), and their meetings take place in nowhere land and help nobody just like the "Nowhere Man" in the famous song by the Beatles — ask any developer, planner, city council member, or county supervisor who's suffered with one or more.

Yet commissioners can help or hinder billions of dollars worth of public and private development every year. If you were explaining the commission system to naked Yap Islanders, as I did, you'd be asked how many years of training are necessary before commissioners are turned loose to do their jobs. In over two decades of meeting with planning commissioners from all over the nation, I've yet to meet one who was adequately prepared beforehand. The operating principle seems to be that lay citizens are **miraculously transubstantiated into learned quasi-judicial regulators and knowledgeable legislative advisors the moment their fannies hit the chair at the first regular meeting.**

Orientation of New Commissioners

After a commissioner knows he or she is going to be appointed, the staff and the chairperson should give this person a general orientation. The staff, or chairperson if there is no staff, should give the new commissioner the accompanying list of the tools of the trade. Each item on this list should be gone over with the new appointee with an explanation of how each is used in the commission's business. After the commissioner has read this material, another briefing session should be scheduled to clear up any questions, misunderstandings, or objections that new commissioner may have. The staff should carefully explain the working relationship between commissioners, planners, and support staff. Issues that should be covered are how the staff goes about developing recommendations and preparing staff reports for the commission's use and the conditions under which commissioners may use additional professional or clerical staff work. The lines of the authority between the staff as employees of the elected body and subordinates of the chief administrator or city manager should be fully understood.

Tools of the Trade for Planning Commissioners

1. A copy of the jurisdiction's general plan and all amendments to it, including a clear statement of community goals or of problems to be addressed through planning and community development.

2. Copies of backup data reports.

3. A base map with a usable scale and sheet size.

4. Copies of regulatory ordinances (zoning, subdivision, sign control, etc.).

5. The agency's budget for the year.

6. The agency's work program for the year. (If there isn't one, find out why.)

7. The commission's bylaws and written procedures.

8. Copies of regional or state policies or programs to which you may be expected to refer on occasion.

9. A copy of any current agreements the planning agency has with other agencies or with consultants.

10. Copies of the rules, regulations, and forms that members of the public receive when they come to the agency for information or permits. (Look at them to see whether they are clear, ensure due process, and are in all cases necessary.)

11. A list of all the maps and reports available and useful for reference if you need them.

The new commissioner should attend a meeting or two as an observer before being sworn in. At such meetings at least the following things should be noted: How do the commissioners work together? Do they talk to each other or mostly to the person taking minutes? How do they arrive at decisions? Do they question staff, applicants, or other people testifying?

What happens when a hearing is closed? Do they go right to a vote or do they tend to take things under advisement until subsequent meetings? After observing the planning staff and commission in action, the new commissioner should again ask penetrating questions about what has been seen and heard. This is no time to be shy about things that may drive him or her up the wall in the long run. For example, one novice noted that although the commission she was going to join met in a hatbox-sized room, everyone on both sides of the table smoked whenever they felt like doing so, which was a lot. After an hour or so, the woman, a nonsmoker, began to feel queasy. Fortunately, she told the chairperson that she had trouble following the proceedings because she couldn't breathe the air in the room and wondered whether smoking could be stopped until breaks. It had never occurred to the men on the commission that smoke-filled rooms were hard for anyone to sit in, much less work in, so they graciously complied. The point of this example is that part of belonging to a group is having members make some allowances for your personal style, whether it's breathing clean air, asking questions, or slowing things down until you're sure you understand what's being acted upon. Belonging is not all subordination. It also includes concessions by the group to allow the increased effectiveness of each individual. So communicate needs early on.

The first thing that new commissioners (and far too many old ones) need to know is how to be effective as a member of a group.

More often than not, a group of average people meeting to make a decision on something will bog down in confusion, aimless bickering, and misunderstanding. Much of the time communication will break down completely and finally all hope of progress on the work at hand dies. Planning commissions fall into this trap. It's necessary to understand a little about the do's and don't's of working together as a group before a commission can expect to be successful with the work itself.

Groups perform two kinds of work. The first is on the external agenda, the tasks that the world expects the group to do. The second kind of work, often overlooked in the struggle to perform the first kind, is the creation and maintenance of the orderly functioning of the group. This is called the "group process."

When a commission is highly involved in internal personality conflicts, game playing, and backbiting, it's called a "process group" and is usually too disorganized to perform its duties well.

Sometimes the commission may be unified, but its energies are diverted to warring with the city council, the chamber of commerce, or other external forces. This group too is probably not getting the primary job done. Only when the commission is organized internally, with its members interacting positively, can it be termed a "work group."

The three standards for gauging whether your commission is functioning as a work group or something else are:

a. **Effectiveness:** Does the commission function as a deliberative study committee, sending up informed advice for the legislative body, or is it mostly a debating society shedding more heat than light on the issues it faces?

b. **Continuity:** Does the commission work toward decisions from a set of principles, the general plan, and policy precedents, or does it fly by the seat of its pants on each new agenda item? The cliché excuse often used when this occurs is: "We aren't bound by anything when a proposal comes in; we consider everything on its merits." A commission functioning as a work group has direction, and each of its decisions is linked to fundamental principles.

c. **Capacity for improvement:** Planning commissions are basically dealing with the problems of growth and change now and in the future. Therefore, as conditions change and new demands are made on the group, it must be able to grow and respond to changing times. A particular challenge to the typical planning commission is the emergence of alternative lifestyles in the community (e.g., communal living groups, halfway houses, etc.) as widespread changes in society continue to occur. A commissioner may find these lifestyles foreign and the people in them personally distasteful, but nevertheless he or she should consider their needs and proposals with care, sensitivity, and a desire not to let personal feelings get in the way of fair and objective decisions on their behalf.

If a commission lacks these prerequisites for functioning as a work group, then it may begin to fall apart and ultimately die. Three symptoms signal the decay of a nonfunctional commission. These are:

Loss of spirit: The members may feel so little need to keep the commission going that they first become apathetic and then drift away until it literally falls apart from lack of participation.

Physical decay: Physical disintegration and finally paralysis may be brought on by prolonged absenteeism, an inept chairperson who makes a mess of things, or some other circumstance that makes the commission less and less effective. Finally, it may fall so far behind on its work and do so little when it does attempt to catch up that it has to be purged.

Structural disorganization: Disruption by individual feuding or intramural warfare with the council may so disorganize the commission that ultimately its internal structure collapses and it cannot perform very much in the way of useful work on its external agenda.

Chairmanship: A veteran commissioner once said, "A planning commission is like the first stomach of a cow. It predigests material and sends it on to the next stomach to be finally disposed of." However, instead of palatable material, a malfunctioning commission will often pass on a case of indigestion. The key person in the creation and maintenance of a commission that can do an adequate job is the chairperson.

In creating an internal structure, the chairperson is the one in charge of the policing and morale-building apparatus of the group. The essential first step in giving form to an internal group is to adopt a precise and clearly understood set of rules of order (Robert's Rules of Order and a set of bylaws[1] should set up the rules of procedural matters) and a mutually agreed-upon group etiquette. For example, one successful practice that some commissions employ as part of the group etiquette is to have the chairperson poll the members about their opinions and readiness to pass judgment on an agenda item before entertaining any motions to dispose of the matter.

Almost as important as these regulating instruments themselves is how they are made clear to the members, particularly new ones. One method is to have the chairperson or vice-chairperson brief new members on the rules the group has been following,

[1] The bylaws will vary from place to place depending on the details in state enabling legislation and local ordinances creating the planning commission. A sample of bylaws for a planning commission is included as Appendix A.

so they will not be plagued by the all-too-common anxiety over not knowing how to operate acceptably at meetings. Sitting the new member next to a more experienced member so that they form a buddy system team could also reinforce the confidence of a novice commissioner during public meetings by allowing him to ask procedural questions confidentially.

Given a set of rules for structuring the internal form of the group, the chairperson must know how to apply them. How, for example, does he handle the actions of members who tend to disorganize the work of the group? Does he have loyal members of the commission to call up for support in disciplining unruly behavior and keeping members in line? If the chairperson is to carry out the police function of the office he or she must first have group cohesion, which is the product of the morale-building function of the chairperson's office. The test of a group's cohesion is its ability to do a significant amount of work against external pressure, internal agitation, or both. Not only does good morale maximize the amount of work that gets done, but the members' enjoyment from it increases proportionately. Good morale also allows the group to go through periods of extraordinary workloads or pressures in an orderly and effective way.

Long rambling meetings, habitual tabling of items, and perpetual continuances destroy many commissioners' sense of moving ahead. At this point morale plummets. Once this happens, the better commissioners may quit. As one who did put it: "Why give up my free time week after week for meetings where all we do is nitpick and philosophize?"

Because the chairperson is central to the policing and morale-building elements of the group process, he or she should be selected with great care. In concrete terms, how the chairperson performs is central to whether or not boredom, a feeling of wasting one's time, and frustration over not getting the work done will set in among the rest of the commission. Despite this fact, the job is often casually rotated among the members of a commission like turns at bat in a baseball game. The best commissioner for the job should serve as chairperson. Commissioners who can serve as even minimally effective chairpersons must have the following characteristics:

a. The chairperson must be strong enough to make sure meetings are run by the rules but fair enough to be above

63

cutting people off before they've had their say or squelching arguments he doesn't agree with. In other words, the chairperson's gavel should be wielded by someone who can use his power properly.

b. The chairperson should have the ability to grasp the whole problem before the commission and not let the main purpose get sidetracked into details. On any given item, she must retain her sense of perspective well enough to avoid the game of far too many commissions, *making big ones out of little ones.*

c. The chairperson should have some aptitude for bridging differences on the commission and bringing matters to a decision. One of the chief ways to do this is by discerning whether the differences are over fundamental principles or are merely disagreements about the means to the end. Once this is done, the chairperson should operate on the premise that while principles should rarely be compromised, means to an end are eminently compromisable. Therefore, if it's clear that commissioners stand apart only on the method involved in achieving the same end, the chairperson ought to try to find common ground before calling for a divisive yes or no vote, for planning is not a game played for winning or losing.

d. The chairperson should also be an effective representative of the commission to other groups, most of all the group of elected officials the commission is advising.

Group adjustment to working effectively requires that each member receive a minimum amount of stimulation and structured work time (provided by the chairperson) to feel that his or her time and energy devoted to commission work are rewarding and useful. Moreover, each member should enjoy a tension-free and comfortable feeling within the group so that no one will feel inhibited about discussions and asking questions. Many new commissioners have confessed a reluctance to ask questions such as, "What's the difference between a variance and a conditional use permit?" They were inhibited because they still felt uncomfortable within the group and feared speaking up with a question would somehow make them seem ignorant.

Finally, if everything in internal functioning of the group is well adjusted, work on the external agenda can begin. Here the goal is to bring each member into the commission's work at his or her highest level. A member may be working at one of the following four levels:

1. **Participation:** Anyone who either gives off or responds to stimuli is participating. However, he may be participating by ritual-predictable behavior, where all a member may do is to second any and all motions "to get them on the floor for discussion" but without ever joining in the discussion. Or he may be serving on the commission just as a way of passing the time—a pastime. If commissioners are just putting in their time by ducking controversy and making ringing speeches on good government and the need for good planning, they may be simply trying to make a record that will be a springboard to higher offices.

2. **Involvement:** This is a commissioner (usually new) who's taking a passive role in the game of another member. (A game is defined as an ulterior transaction in which people try to manipulate others to bring on a desired response.) For example, a commissioner identified with real estate interests may manipulate a new member from the local homeowners' group by pointing out that the development to be approved will lower property taxes, raise resale prices, and provide the homeowners' children a place to play. He might say something like: "How could anyone want homeowners to miss out on such a good deal? Are you for or against these kinds of things for your people, Joe?" He'll ask before Joe has had a chance to check on whether the proposed benefits would really occur; and often one more vote is neatly harpooned by the game.[2]

3. **Engagement:** A commissioner who takes the initiative in starting his or her own games or actively tries to steer someone else's game to his or her advantage is operating actively and is *engaged*

4. **Belonging:** When an individual has given up manipulative games and begins to play it the commission's way (objectively and for the broader interests of the community), then he or she *belongs* and is fully functional as a planning commissioner.

[2] Although commissioners do not appoint themselves, the myth that "the proper mix" on the commission ought to be various representatives of special constituencies (business, homeowners, young minorities, commuters, old timers, etc.) still persists. The best mix on a commission is as many people with broad-gauged, objective outlooks as can be found. A good commissioner represents the best interests of the entire community when issues arise. To the extent that a commissioner is tied to special interests, the community as a whole loses out. The "proper mix" is therefore a collection of commissioners judicious enough to "belong."

Groupthink: Some years ago Irving L. Janis,[3] in analyzing the decision-making processes that preceded such debacles as the Bay of Pigs invasion and the Vietnam War, coined this term to represent the surrender of individual intelligence to the illusions of a group. Commissions that "go along" to "get along" often exhibit the following symptoms when they meet to decide on something:

a. An unquestioned elitist belief in the inherent "rightness" and morality of their decisions, regardless of the effects on others or on the future.[4]

b. Fixed ideas of developers as crooks, renters as transient undesirables, nonresidents as second-class citizens, businessmen as evil profiteers, newcomers as threats to "our way of life," etc., etc. These people are therefore not listened to objectively or considered worth a genuine attempt to negotiate with over differences.

c. Often there is strong pressure from politicians as well as others on the commission on any commissioner who deviates from the group's views, commitments, or stereotyped beliefs. Doubts, public questioning, and dissent are considered disloyal and censored.

d. A push from the majority to make all decisions unanimous. Often in such groups, the chairperson will force things through by announcing that silence means consent.

e. Mind guarding and censorship of staff by chairpersons, chief administrators, mayors, and planning directors to shield commissioners from information that might sidetrack

---

[3] Irving L. Janis, *Victims of Groupthink* (Boston: Houghton Mifflin Co., 1972).

[4] Not only governmental groups are afflicted by groupthink. John Z. DeLorean's look inside the top management decisions at General Motors when he became a member of that elite executive team was "At General Motors the concern for the effect of our products on our many publics was never discussed except in terms of cost or sales potential. And being a member of the management team meant you supported your boss's decisions, even if you thought they were wrong. When you opposed your superiors, you were accused of 'not being on the team.'" On the approval of the unsafe Corvair car, he reports: "These were not immoral men who were bringing out this car. These were warm breathing men with families and children who as private individuals would never have approved this project for a minute if they were told 'You are going to kill and injure people with this car.' But these same men in a business atmosphere where everything is reduced to terms of costs, profit goals, and production deadlines, were able as a group to approve a product most of them wouldn't have considered approving as individuals." Quoted from J. Patrick Wright, *On a Clear Day You Can See General Motors* (New York: Avon Books, 1979), p. 6.

them from reaching the desired decision or shatter their complacency about the effectiveness and correctness of their decisions.

f. In some commissions, members will censor themselves to send up decisions that are "what the people who appointed me want."

Decision making: Once the internal structure of a commission is in place, it should be able to reach decisions effectively. Most believe that decisions should always be reached by polling the members under majority-rules voting procedures. This is the model, but it does have some pitfalls that should be avoided. One is a feeling by members on the short end of a vote that there wasn't enough time for them to get their point of view across — that the majority votes were there and their views were just a waste of time. This breeds resentment and often withdrawal from discussions. An advanced stage of this problem is the creation of permanent factions in win-lose competition with each other, especially if there's a swing vote to be won. In majority-rules decision making, the minority must be made to feel that they have been given fair treatment and that their views are respected and could be part of a majority opinion next time. No one wants to be on a commission where he or she is permanently relegated to the losing side on every vote.

Some groups take the extra time to reach a consensus. In this method, communication is carried on in a supportive climate so that everyone feels he or she has had a fair chance to affect the decision. Then the chairperson will call for a test motion reflecting the "sense of the discussion" and lay it open to more discussion and amending. A consensus is not unanimity, but a psychological state where those not in full agreement are able to go along with the decision because they feel that their alternative has been understood and that they have been given sufficient opportunity to sway the others to their position.

Some poorer methods of decision making abound. The most common are listed here:

a. **Scatterbrainstorming:** Every time someone offers an idea, someone else offers another before the first one is discussed. The result is nonsupport of an idea by bypassing it until the group finds one it likes. It leaves the proposer with the feeling

67

of having put a half-dead fish on the table — to wriggle and die while others ignore it. This lack of simple courtesy soon kills the initiative of more reticent members.

b. **Looking to authority:** Many groups make decisions in response to an authority figure. Some commissions blindly follow the lead of the planner. Sometimes they are set up to let the chairperson or the ex officio member from the city council tell them what the right decision will be. While this is efficient, it requires too little involvement for any real commitment to the decision to take place.

c. **Railroading:** Often there is a clique on the commission who can force decisions without the real consent of the majority. They come up with a motion before anyone can discuss the issues and ram it through. The chairperson is usually instrumental in railroading decisions through, using such ploys as "It's late and we've all heard the facts on this, so let's vote and move on," or "Most of us know how we want to move on this," assuming the intimidated silence of some commissioners to mean consent. Such cabals leave other members — often a majority — feeling alienated and resentful. Eventually a revolt may take place when the majority learns that they've been manipulated by a minority.

Skills of a good planning commissioner: People who serve on planning commissions should be selected on the basis of the following criteria:

a. **Civic-mindedness:** It helps if the commissioner already has a track record for working on civic programs such as neighborhood or downtown improvement projects.

b. **An interest in planning** and enough knowledge of the planning process and laws to know why things are done as well as the rules for doing them.

c. **A mind open to new ideas:** A person who will be working with change and the future should have the imagination and flexibility to grasp, evaluate, and accept new ideas.

d. **Objectivity:** An ability to listen to opposing views and still keep a clear focus on where the real public interest lies, what is not only within the law but also really fair, and if possible, a judicial temperament in the face of controversy — namely, the ability to distinguish between fact and opinion.

e. **The ability to express oneself clearly and concisely in public:** This includes the skill of learning to think on your feet, something very few of us learned in school.

f. **Enough free time to adequately prepare for meetings:** Making decisions on planning matters is hard enough without having to play catchup at meetings. It's not fair to those concerned, as well as the community you're supposed to serve, to constantly try to "play things by ear."

g. **No conflicts of interest:** This means avoiding not only a mixing of public service and private gain, but also the making of a decision on the basis of who's involved rather than what.

Once a qualified commissioner goes to work, some of the most important skills to be used or acquired are:

a. **The ability to define what's at issue on any matter requiring a decision:** It's vital to know beforehand what it is you have to decide. A good planner will give you guidance on what the main issues are on any matter and the options before you in making a decision.

b. **The ability to assemble information from both written and oral testimony and to apply it to the making of meaningful recommendations for the people you advise:** Recommendations should rely more on adopted plans and policies than on personal values.

c. **The ability to take an initiative in policy issues:** Good commissioners should be able to do more for their communities than react to what's placed before them on the regular meeting agenda. For example, if a new type of development or trend emerges for which a breathing spell is needed to find answers, a good commission will take the initiative in stopping the permit machinery until it has the answers.

d. **The ability to keep the long view:** Good commissioners will develop a sense of how things that are done now will affect the future of the community, especially the people who will one day be residents but haven't arrived yet. These people are the special constituency of planning commissions.

Making the commission more effective: Far too many commissions are overwhelmed by the work they are required to do and feel, like Alice, that they must run as fast as they can just to keep from losing ground. Here are a few ideas others have tried with real success to increase effectiveness:

a. **Delegate:** Many small items such as setback variances, special permits, and exceptions, which clutter up meeting agendas, can be handled administratively by staff. Many communities use a zoning administrator for such matters. In states where the legal requirements for making a record and setting forth findings are complex, hearings officers have been handling zone changes, planned unit developments, and complex project reviews as well.

b. **Improve your planning knowledge:** There are many courses, conferences, and special workshops that offer nuts-and-bolts training for commissioners. Many communities have set up special one- or two-day training sessions for commissioners, staff, and anyone else in local government who may benefit from such classes. Importing special trainers is often less expensive than sending commissioners and staff to national conferences held in expensive hotels clear across the nation.

c. **Look beyond the meeting room:** Attend the meetings of other nearby planning commissions to see what you can learn from how they do their work. Invite staff from other cities, the county, the metro or council of governments' planning agency, and state and federal bureaus to give firsthand accounts of new programs, projects, laws, and regulatory devices, including new court decisions affecting planning.

d. **Take stock:** Get out in the community for field trips *after* a project has been built as well as before. Did it come off as proposed or are there a whole set of problems that were overlooked? How can you do it better next time?

Have at least one meeting per year for a review of where you've been as a commission, where you're headed (work programs), and what you'll need to improve your community's planning next year. Suggestions could be anything from a more reliable tape recorder for meetings to a streamlined amendment review and adoption process. Review the goals and policies you've been working under. Are they being achieved? Do they still make sense or do you need something more practical? For example, does your plan have an agenda that won't work under the new conditions of fiscal austerity in government? What should be retained? What should be restructured (deferred, reduced, relocated, recycled)? What should be developed? For some communities, removal of the rosy tints from their general plans is a matter of urgent priority if they are to be left with anything to work with in the leaner times ahead.

Intramural Coordinating or the Art of Not Passing the Buck

5

In passing the buck, we give up local control. From here on out, if we fill out all the forms on schedule, do as we are told, and mark all documents to show they were financially aided through a federal grant, we get enough of our money back from the feds to do some of the things we couldn't afford to do with our money if we had to raise it at home . . . . But now somehow we can *afford them. We won! But now we dislike the results of our victory.*

— Fred Bair
Planning Cities

Once the commission has its own internal structure taken care of, it still faces a considerable task in developing a positive relationship with its staff, the city council or board of supervisors, administrators, and other departments and agencies that influence or implement planning.

Staff: Assuming that the commission receives the services of a professional planner and his or her staff, the first question that arises is that of a proper working relationship. Should the commission consider itself the boss of the planners on the payroll, despite the fact that public-administration texts teach future city managers that the planning function is a staff operation closer to administrative operations than advisory groups like planning commissions? Adding to the vagueness of the lines of authority over the staff is the fact that the council members or supervisors consider the professional planners their employees, especially at budget time. In addition, in many jurisdictions it is the legislative body, not the commission, that hires and fires planning directors. Yet most of a planner's work will be with the planning commission.

71

The best answer to the dilemma of how can a planner serve two or more masters is, *don't make him do it*. The commission should instead consider itself the planner's principal client. The legislative officers should be recognized as the ones who generate policy and exercise budgetary control over most of the work that goes on in a jurisdiction. The administrator should be viewed as the one responsible for seeing that their policies are carried out and their budgetary limits are respected. With this in mind, the commission should not assume that it can unilaterally generate major chores for the staff, such as a complete overhaul of the zoning ordinance. On the other hand, a commission shouldn't turn its staff loose to do anything it wants to do. Administrative chores such as proper processing of zoning and subdivision applications, sending notices of public hearings, clear and adequate staff reports, arranging the meeting place, taking care of commission minutes, correspondence, and records are all responsibilities that should be delegated to a staff.

A commission should not attempt to handle the small details of policy and decision making. They should not be afraid, as so many commissions are, of delegating authority. For example, much of the fuss and bother of variances, conditional use permits, design review, lot splits, and minor development plan revisions can and should be handled administratively, with cases not settled by staff coming to the legislative body on appeal.[1] The commission should also be flexible about staff interpretation of standards and requirements such as the information required from an applicant.

The staff should be able to plan its own annual work program and budget. The commission should review, comment, and suggest improvements in terms of its own work. Program budgets that describe how much each category or major item

[1] Processing of variances, conditional use permits, negative declarations, etc. could be handled by an ordinance creating a zoning administrator. He should be responsible for noticing and holding public hearings and making findings of unnecessary hardship in strict compliance with the intent of the zoning ordinance. He should be responsible for interpreting the ordinance to the public, referring legal questions to lawyers. Proposals that involve changes in land use or policy should not be handled at this level, but should be referred to the commission.

of work is going to cost are much better for planning work than line-item budgets that only list how many pencils, typists, and maps the planning department would like to acquire next year. When cuts in a proposed planning budget are considered (and they always are), it's better to make the budget-cutters own up to their cuts in terms of planning product deferred than to let them get away with the old bromide, "You ought to be able to do all that with fewer people and less money." Priority ratings as well as costs are helpful in deciding what must be funded and what might wait. *Remember, unless there is adequate financing, planning becomes wishful thinking by a discussion group.* A good planning program not only produces recommendations about the action that should be taken but has enough follow-through to see that the action *is* taken.

During the course of the year (every three months at a minimum), the commission should make time for and insist on periodic progress reports by staff on non-day-to-day items such as plan preparation, ordinance writing, rezoning studies, and surveys. These reports should include a summary of funds and man-hours expended to date, percentage of work completed, work to be done before the next periodic report, and estimated time to completion. Elaborate presentations and reports should be discouraged; they are all too often bureaucratic and self-serving smoke screens.

Estimates of working time should be treated rather charitably because it's very difficult to predict the number of man-hours needed to complete a given planning project. Such a project is quite unlike a paving or vaccination project: no one really knows how long it will take a planner to think through problems that are essentially without precedent and often without standard procedure.

Nevertheless, as far as possible, deadlines should be considered as necessary evils, and unless there is some overriding reason to do otherwise the staff should be expected to adhere to them. This should also serve to curb the tendency of many planners to keep on compiling data, hopping from one completed survey to the next research phase and endlessly postponing the day when there's a completed project that can be put to practical use. As a rule, prolonged research projects are not suited to the needs and resources of local government.

When to replace your planner: While commissions rarely hire the planner, as the principal client they may be in the best position to see the need for a change in personnel. A commission should not tolerate for very long a planner

☐ who can't plan, but is merely a paper shuffler;

☐ who goes off half-cocked in public or is a disorganized prima donna who voices opinions rather than producing evidence;

☐ who can't run the department, as evidenced by fouled-up public hearing notices and applications, and incomplete, incoherent, or inaccurate staff reports;

☐ who is unsympathetic to the community and the groups that live and work in it;

☐ who can't work with interest groups in the community without being unduly loyal or attached to one or another;

☐ who is a publicity seeker and detracts from the dignity and credibility of the planning function by making extreme statements or by indulging in bizarre behavior to gain this publicity;

☐ who becomes the spokesperson for the commission on matters on which it has yet to take a position;

☐ who has any financial interest in any development within the jurisdiction for which he or she works.

On the other side of the coin are the responsibilities of a commission toward its staff. A partial list would include:

☐ Allowing the planner to state his professional opinions even if they clash with those of the commission. Never muzzle your staff. The commission, in fact, should be in the vanguard of his defense if he's attacked for legitimate actions connected with the planning operation of the jurisdiction he serves.

☐ He should not be used as a scapegoat or cat's paw in political disputes. In essence, he should not be ordered to find that a proposal is technically "good or bad" after minds have been made up on political grounds. Nor should the commission hide behind the planner if a decision it has made proves unpopular. It's foul play to say, "We (the commission) voted the way we did because the planner slanted the facts."

☐ He should be introduced by the commissioners to the people and organizations he'll need to know in order to understand the community. Commissioners are usually better public escorts for planners than elected officials, because the latter's public appearances are so often interpreted as vote-gathering or political fence-mending visits. (They often are.) This compromises the planner and may make his professional objectivity suspect in the opposition camp.

☐ The commission should work only through the planning director in seeking information or services from anyone in his department. Bypassing the director at any time undermines the organization and operation of his department. This is a major problem in some places where the director is new and the staff isn't.

☐ The planner must be working with the commission on a basis of confidence, goodwill, and trust.

Working with a consultant: The best way to utilize a planning consultant is as a supplement to the permanent staff, adding his or her specialties to the staff's general knowledge of the community and its problems. Ideally the product of a consultant's employment should be more than a report. The experience should leave behind an upgraded staff ready to carry on the work and competent to explain the consultant's work to the rest of the community. Sometimes the community may not have a professional staff. When this is the case, the commission will have to work more closely with the consultant and give direction, particularly with reference to local feelings and attitudes. The consultant is, after all, a stranger in town. A commission, for this reason, can't delegate as much authority to a consultant as it would a resident staff planner.

At the outset of the decision to employ a consultant, the specific services that are going to be needed should be carefully set out in writing. If the commission feels unequal to the task, in most states it can get professional assistance from the state office of planning, from the nearest college or university that has a planning faculty, from the nearest office of the federal Department of Housing and Urban Development, or from the regional planning agencies that contain the local jurisdiction that needs help. Any of these government agencies[2] can supply the names of consultants. A few of the

[2] The national office of the American Planning Association, 1776 Massachusetts Avenue N.W., Washington, D.C., may also be consulted for names of consul-

consultants on a list, never more than eight to ten, should be sent a statement of the specific services that are going to be required and an invitation to submit a written proposal on how they would perform the services. A list of all the jobs they've had in the last five years should also be required.

Choosing the consultant: At this point, the locality is in somewhat the same fix as the man who advertised for a mail order bride and now has to make a choice from among several alluring replies. There is one important difference, however: the planning consultant has had previous liaisons that can and should be checked out. Call three or four of the consultant's most recent clients and get on-the-level answers to the following questions:

a. Has the work the consultant did been useful to the clients since he left?

b. Did the services he performed meet the expectations of the clients, or do they feel that they were left with a poorer product than they had reason to expect?

c. Would the clients have this consultant back to do more work without qualifications, or would they look elsewhere first?

Throw away the responses from those consultants whose work has not been useful, who produced something less than what the client bargained for, and who wouldn't be allowed back for more work. Now read the responses of those who have passed the references test with the following criteria in mind:

a. Does the proposal get to the point about why this particular consultant is a good bet to do these specific services? Or does the response come in the form of a self-serving advertising brochure about how great this firm is, without mention of how it would deal with the unique problems of your community?

b. What's the style of the response? Is it clear and relevant to what was requested? Is it free of flashy packaging and technical doubletalk, and open about who the firm has available to work on this project and what their qualifications are? Watch out for firms that promise more talent than a major

tants. For fuller particulars on what consultants recommend as a selection procedure, read *Selecting a Professional Planning Consultant and Administration of the RFP*, available from the American Society of Consulting Planners, 1750 Old Meadow Road, McLean, Virginia 22101.

film studio but show in the fine print that most of their "stars" are only bound to them by a loose agreement to share fees on a subcontract basis. This may mean that the firm responding is essentially a brain brokerage operation with little real responsibility for the overall quality of the work that gets farmed out.

After making the appropriate cuts, the most promising two or three consultants should be called in for a face-to-face interview with a consultant selection panel. It should include the planning director, representatives of each faction of the planning commission, the city council or board of supervisors, and the chairperson of the citizens' study committee, if there is one.[3] The interview should be with the person who will captain the job.

The consultant should then be asked:

a. What special qualifications his team would bring to the task if his firm were hired? (Be specific about determining who is going to be working on the program.)

b. How will he do the work and how will the final product be used by the community?

Avoid competitive bidding, "loss leader" services by firms that will provide planning below cost to get their foot in the door for more lucrative public works or construction bids, or any other form of cut-rate pricing. Inquiries with other jurisdictions should establish the cost range of the desired consulting services. It's no sin to let the consultant know the budgetary range he'll be working in before he prepares his proposal. He should really know at the selection interview pretty much what he can do for the money or he should be prepared to present a strong case as to why more will be needed. A consultant should be chosen on the basis of who will do the best job, not

---

[3] When a major planning project is launched, such as a downtown or comprehensive plan, citizen participation in the form of a special committee is generally viewed as valuable because the representative citizens' group can serve as an informed sounding board for the proposals that the program generates; it can carry the planning message to interested community groups by serving as liaison between the official government sponsors of the program and the citizens' organizations that will be affected by the plans. Finally, such a task force can be a positive force at public hearings for adoption of planning proposals. Once the purpose of such a special group has been fulfilled, it should be disbanded.

who will charge the least. A really good consultant, once hired, may be able to design a tighter program than his client had in mind and thereby effect real savings all around; but the negotiations as to exactly what the consultant will produce for a specific amount of money should take place after he's been selected but not yet under contract. That's the time to lay all the cards on the table and make sure that everyone concerned knows what's going to be produced by the consultant, and, more important, how it will be used.

Finally, don't be afraid of instincts. Even though things look good on paper, if the consultant the selection panel is interviewing still seems too slick or hard to understand, then he might be wrong for this particular place, even though he has plenty of qualifications. Get the consultant who comes through most clearly and who seems personally suited to working with your community. When the consultant's agreement is drawn, leave some money for services on a retainer basis so that he can help implement his proposals. For communities without a staff, retention of the consultant after the work is finished is essential.

The legislators: The most important thing to remember about the commission's relationship with the elected politicians who appointed it is that while the commission is to study, prepare plans, review and advise on development proposals, *it does not act.* Not having the final say is a hard thing for many commissioners to swallow. Why go on expending great amounts of time and energy sending up advice to people who may not follow it or even consider it? One compensation for the commission that has a low batting average with the city fathers is the fact that as the commissioners make their recommendations known, they are also offering informed advice and alternatives to the public and to agencies that will play a role in resolving an issue.

In some jurisdictions the commissioners are supposed to resign after each election or when there's a new majority on the legislative body. This is supposed to ensure that the new legislators/majority get a chance to pick their people. Loyalty to the legislative body, however, is not as important as getting the best minds to serve. Since local government legislative bodies are usually not subject to the checks and balances of equally powerful judicial and executive branches, some intelligent dissent between a commission and its elected bosses may be healthy for the community as a whole. Independent commissioners with staggered terms to ensure continuity would therefore seem to be the better way to organize a local planning commission.

However, the commission exists to help the council or supervisors do a better job of acting on planning matters. The commission should add an extra dimension to the deliberations of the legislators, namely, concern for the future. This is where reference to a comprehensive plan is vital.

Another key attribute of a good commission is that it can bring about coordination. For example, this kind of commission can achieve cooperation and coordination on things like subdivision review between planning and other departments such as public works, health, and parks. In some cases other agencies, such as special districts (sewer, water, utilities, and flood control) and the school district, neighboring jurisdictions, and housing authorities with their own powers of implementation, have been brought together so that the city or county will have the benefit of prior comprehensive review of a development for its own deliberations. If the commission's decisions are shaped by these acts of coordination with other departments and agencies they should carry much more weight with the legislators than if they were made in isolation. Lining up the opinion on a matter or at least clearly defining what's at issue before sending up a recommendation is the best way for a commission to capture the legislators' respect and attention. To be most effective, a commission should have periodic meetings with the legislators so that matters of joint policy and direction are mutually understood and if possible agreed upon.

Legislative bodies need more than a yes or no vote tally when they receive a commission recommendation. They need the pertinent facts (don't bury them in petty details) and good solid reasons for doing what the commission recommends. These reasons must be set down in writing and sent along before the public meeting when the legislators take up the matter passed on by the commission.

Compatibility with the general plan is the best way to assess the long-range implications, options, and readjustments that passing a proposal will bring about. The plan, therefore, should be used as a foil for development of the reasons for commission recommendations on current development proposals.

In sending up its advice and information, the commission could find itself differing with its staff on a particular subject. Problems could occur when the planner is asked to present both the staff's position and the commission's. When staff and commission disagree, a commissioner should present his group's side of the issue if at all possible and leave the staff planner free to advocate his position, rather than have him attempt to appear to be giving equal weight to conflicting sets of recommendations.

A final observation on coordinating with the elected politicians—when giving advice, it's much better to be asked for it than to volunteer it. There are good reasons the upper body should ask for this advice. Among the major ones is the fact that by having controversial issues aired first by a planning commission, the elected politicians provide a buffer or safety valve for themselves against pressure groups, bureaucratic empire builders, and proposals that may or may not be politically feasible.

Administrators: In many jurisdictions the planning commission and staff are extremely useful to the administrator as interdepartmental coordinators. This is done in three main ways:

a. By focusing each department's development review procedures on the commission's regulatory processes (public hearings, approvals, appeals, and environmental impact reports).

b. By reviewing departmental proposals involving any physical change in the community (roads, public buildings, parks, flood channels, and public housing) in the light of its effects on the community at large (traffic generation, environmental impacts, neighborhood disruption, and population growth). Many jurisdictions require the commission to report on whether public project proposals conform to the provisions of local general plans (e.g., the federal grant review at the regional level, named "A-95 clearinghouse review").

c. By coordinating each public development proposal with short-range fiscal and administrative priorities as well as longer-range planning objectives. This occurs when the commission is in charge of reviewing the local capital improvement program for conformity with the general plan. If the commission does this task thoroughly, it will be in a very good position to determine when one department or agency's plans are on a collision course with another's. More positively, it can suggest joint actions that would be mutually beneficial. For example, the commission could recommend that the playground-park site that the parks department wishes to buy be combined with the purchase of the new school site programmed for acquisition by the school district, and that the playground facilities be planned for joint use in order to make each tax dollar buy more.

The smart administrator knows that he will benefit from having interdepartmental competition and political lobbying moved away from the doorstep and onto a neutral ground such as the planning commission. With the commission, each public proposal can be appraised objectively, publicly, and thoroughly, but not, thank goodness, finally, for that would close too many options when the issue becomes political again.

City or county attorneys: Finally, there is one other person on the civic roster who needs special mention — the commission's legal counsel. The basic rule on the use of counsel is: when in doubt about how to proceed legally, stop the procedural wheels until you can get a legal opinion. Counsel's first job is to keep the enemy out of the commission's camp. Sometimes a hearing may have to be continued until counsel clears up such mundane matters as whether proper legal notice was received. At other times, he or she may need to work closely with staff in drawing up a legal instrument for growth control — exactions of open space or fees from developers, or how to regulate a new use for which the zoning ordinance makes no provision. When a very controversial proposal that may lead to litigation is being considered, counsel should be at the meeting in order to control the legal circumstances of a case he or she may have to defend in court. It is not usually necessary to have counsel at every meeting. If the action of the commission may be questioned in court, it would be wise to review with counsel the wording of the findings supporting the action the commission wishes to take.

When litigation is a possibility, greater care must be taken in making and keeping records of the entire proceeding. The commission and its staff should be sure to send out hearing notices by registered mail, to take a transcript of the testimony during the hearing that will be admissible in court, and to hang on to all maps, petitions, letters, and other material evidence introduced. The directions of commission counsel should be followed closely in such situations.

Finally, counsel should be the commission's primary source person on new state planning and zoning legislation, applicable new ordinances adopted in other jurisdictions, and court decisions that have a bearing on the operations and scope of the commission's duties and responsibilities.

Public Meetings and Public Relations

6

*When I, the People learn to
    remember, when I the
People use the lessons of
    yesterday and no longer
forget who robbed me last
    year, who played me for
a fool—then there will be
    no speaker in all the world
say the name "The People"
    with any fleck of a
sneer in his voice or any
    far off smile of derision,
the mob—the crowd—the
    mass will arrive then.*
                —Carl Sandburg
                    "The People, Yes"

The planning commission in any community has a responsibility to inform and educate the public about the purposes of
planning. The commission should also report on how the
specific problems about which people are concerned are being
resolved. In many cities, especially the smaller ones, planning
and development proposals stir up more public clamor than
any other governmental activity. Good public relations are
therefore vital for a planning commission. Without public
opinion on its side, the commission's recommendations will
lack the kind of support that is required to hurdle the inevitable
political opposition of those who would gain from having
things go the other way. As Fred Bair put it:

The first responsibility of the public planner is to the public, present and future, and to the greater public ... so the planner's public is broad in its generality. It is also deep. There is a lesson to be learned from a Nigerian chief who said, 'My people are a family in which some are dead, a few are here and many are coming'. ... Serving the general public, the planner's supreme boss, isn't easy because the part of the general public which happens to be on the scene isn't much interested in what happens to the larger part of the general public which isn't there yet. **One of the defects of democracy is that the unborn can't vote.** *The planner must plead their cause for them and it isn't easy.*[1]

However, the planner's unborn constituency can't be reached for its opinions. This requires that the message of planning should reach as broad a cross section of the "living" public as possible. Its preferences and reactions should be reasonably balanced against the needs of the unborn in making planning decisions. The commission's special tools for successful public relations are information about what has been happening (how much growth, how fast it's coming, how land is being used, and how much housing is available). The commission also needs to respond to the people's expectations for the future. The only way planning can make sense to ordinary citizens is to show them how the changes they see going on now are going to fit together. It is to be hoped that the current changes will fit future aspirations well enough so that the public can have decent expectations about its future in terms of its amenities, its property, its safety, and its children's welfare. Contacts with the public should communicate as much as possible about current programs and problems. They should also seek out and answer criticism. (For example, why is the commission approving so many apartments, mobile home parks, gas stations, fast food stands, and condominiums?)

The planning director and articulate members of the staff should have the skills to reach the public in this way as speakers to local groups, as authors of reports, and in contacts with the press and other media. Nevertheless, the commission

[1] Fred H. Bair, Jr., *Planning Cities* (Chicago: American Society of Planning Officials, 1970), pp. 48–49.

should have its own spokespersons, preferably the chairperson who has authority to speak for the commission about its views, what it did, and why it did it. The chair should also be accessible to reporters at reasonable hours and have authority for news releases.

A good commission should have several members who circulate among the people in the community, getting the public pulse and the kind of public opinion that can't be gauged in the tumult of public hearings. People should be consulted on their basic special interests as homeowners, businessmen, parents, farmers. Let them talk on the level of "what's going to happen to me and mine," rather than asking them what they think of the options for a citywide design for the year 2000.

There has been a growing trend to give citizens' groups a role in planning. In working out goals and policy recommendations, they can be both helpful and a threat to the proper functioning of a planning commission. The goal of active citizen partici- pation in public planning has long been government gospel, but exactly what it is supposed to accomplish has not always been clear.

Frequently, citizens' planning committees may be appointed to augment the official planning commission; they are put to work on demanding and complex projects such as a compre- hensive plan, an open space program, or a number of neighborhood improvement programs. These committees study the problems, listen to the information prepared by the staff, and prepare findings and policy recommendations for submission to the elected officials. Because they are also playing an advisory role, such citizens' committees can become a freewheeling duplication of, or worse yet an end run around, the planning commission. To avoid this and to ensure close coordination with such committees, the following steps should be taken by the commission:

☐ A close working relationship between the commission, the staff, and the citizens' committee should be spelled out at the very beginning. It is highly desirable to have at least two commissioners appointed to serve on the committee and act as a two-way communication conduit between the com- mission and the committee.

☐ The committee should present its findings and recommendations to the planning commission as a whole and the commission should be given time for review and comment. If there are disagreements between commission and committee, a commission report should accompany the committee's report to the legislative body.

☐ The committee should serve only during the period of the committee's project and thereafter it should be thanked and promptly disbanded.

The most important aspect of a planning commission's public relations is its public meetings. Winfred Winholtz has described the following eight elements of a successful meeting:

Purpose: It may be belaboring the obvious, but there should be a good reason for calling any meeting. The chairman should have a clear idea as to what he wants to get out of a meeting, and should make this purpose known to the participants. The purpose of a hearing may be just to receive the views of interested parties; the purpose of a commission meeting may be to consider reports and read decisions on certain matters; the purpose of a staff conference may be simply to pass on information.

Notice: Don't expect people to show up if you haven't invited them and given them some clue as to why they should come. Whether this is by word of mouth, office memo, engraved invitation, or legal advertisement depends, of course, on the nature of the affair. Those who will have important roles to play should get special attention and reminders. This would apply particularly to prospective supporters who seldom appear at public hearings without prompting.

Preparations: These have to do not only with arrangements for the meeting place, food, supplies, comforts, visual aids, transportation and such mechanical things, but also with the agenda, content, reports, rehearsals, and arrangements for people to do certain things either for or at the meeting. The important feature of all preparations is that they must be done in advance. The time of the meeting should be set to allow for adequate preparations.

Agenda: Without an agenda or order of business, a meeting is not a meeting, it is a "happening" with no guarantee that it will come off well. Even a public hearing needs clear and fair rules as to the sequence and procedure to be followed. The partici-

pants need to know that there is a place when they will "get their chance." If copies of the agenda are not available for everyone, then it is important for the chairman to describe it at the start of the meeting and to justify any variation from it.

Participants: The most important participant is the man up front—the chairman—to whom the others are looking for direction in the progress of the meeting. His bearing and attitude can influence more than any single factor the outcome of a meeting or hearing. His patience may be taxed, but his application of the principles of fairness in the conduct of the meeting should not waiver.

Other participants will at times include both leaders and followers, friends and foes, helpmates and agitators, table-thumpers and sitters-on-hands. Their diversity is too great to treat here, other than to note that most successful meetings are not monologues. Participants is a plural word.

Place: The meeting place selected should be a comfortable, convenient one appropriate to the size and nature of the meeting to be held. There may be times when nothing can be done about a dimly lighted or poorly ventilated hall, but there is no valid excuse for not checking facilities beforehand and making the best use of them. Few things are more disruptive of a meeting than the microphone that doesn't work or the visual aid that can't be seen.

Results: Something comes of every meeting, although it may not always be readily evident. Even fruitless sessions create impressions and contribute to the development of attitudes over time. But the kinds of meetings we want are the productive ones, which can be summarized at their close with findings, agreements, decisions. Most meetings are not ends in themselves, but steps or means. The results of these frequently are work assignments, tasks to be done and reported on at the next meeting. No meeting is really finished until its results are stated and the next steps made clear.

Records: Seldom does everyone who should come to a meeting show up. For this reason if no other, some record should be made in order that the missing participants may be informed. More importantly, most planning work is public, and the public interest calls for certain types of records. These range from the verbatim transcript or tape recording of public hearing statements, through official published minutes of commission sessions, to much less formal types of records. If *a meeting was worth having, it should have produced a result worth recording. Some planning offices find useful a simple form for listing the time, place, participants, and results of any meeting held. This is intended to be filled out at the end of the meeting, before leaving the meeting room. It can then be reproduced and sent to the participants and to all others who should be informed. Such a minimal record is nice to have as the basis for impressive statistics for annual reports. But it is far more useful as a reminder to follow up on the decisions and assignments made in the meeting.*[2]

Public meetings are the place where most commissions spend the majority of their working time and where their public reputations are made. All too often the impressions the public gets are negative, because the commission commits one or more of the four cardinal sins of running a public meeting:

1. **Not controlling the meeting.** If many people want to speak in a limited time, speaking time should be rationed so all may be heard. Allow speakers for groups more time than random individuals and call on them first. A commonly followed practice is to have the staff present the facts and their recommendations first, then the applicants and their proponents, and then opponents to the proposal. (See Appendix B.) Rebuttals should be allowed only if they present new and relevant factual information for the commission's benefit. Do not allow anyone to filibuster, harangue the audience, deal in personal insults or exchanges, or read long documents like the names on petitions which can just as easily be made part of the record.

   If, for some reason, all sides of an issue can't be heard adequately in the hearing time available, the hearing should be continued to the next meeting. Staff presentations should be short and concise. No interruptions, especially frequent cheering and booing, should be permitted when someone has the floor. The chair should close the hearing and keep it closed to more testimony for proponents and opponents except for questions commissioners may have for anyone who has given testimony.

---

[2] Winfred G. Winholtz, in *Principles and Practice of Urban Planning* (Chicago: International City Managers Association, 1968). Used by permission.

2. **The commission seems unfair.** Commissioners should never bring up the pros and cons of an agenda item before all testimony and evidence have been presented. Then the discussion should stay on the facts presented, not the presenters. Many times commissioners will destroy their objectivity by making personal cracks like, "This developer is the kind of operator I don't want to see building anything in this town, because he's built so much junk in the past," or "This man's a very reliable businessman and I'll believe anything he says without making him bring in a lot of plans and details."

When voting, the commission should be voting for something rather than merely sending up a count of those for and against. *Vote reasons, not opinions.* For example, it's preferable to register a no vote with a statement like, "I'm voting no on this proposal because it clearly violates our general plan and I'm for upholding the plan unless there's a more compelling reason not to than the evidence here shows," rather than, "This is such a lousy development that unless we stop it, it will ruin the town." Don't condemn anyone in public. If there's a question of conflict of interest on the commission, handle it in advance and don't wait for it to come up from the outside, particularly during a public hearing. Consult counsel and a consensus of the commission's conscience on such matters. Not only the direct interests of a commissioner, but those of close relatives and business associates, may pose questions of conflict of interest and should be openly considered as such.

3. **The commission can't bring things to a vote.** Many commissions get so bogged down in petty details, endless searches for new data, and procedural distractions that matters brought before them never seem to get resolved. This is deadly in two ways. First, if the commission is to be responsible as the advisory board to the council or board of supervisors, the commission must wrap things up in a reasonable time. Some commissions have dawdled so long over a proposal that by the time their belated decision reached the next level of government deliberation the applicants were able to point out that conditions had changed in the community since the commission first took evidence on the matter and that its findings were therefore obsolete. If the applicant is a developer, unreasonable delays can be ruinous to his prospects of

completion of a project. Denial by inaction is the worst kind of injustice to a businessman who will suffer severe financial loss from the unnecessary stalling of a legitimate proposal.

The commission should learn the art of proposing and amending motions that capture the common ground of the majority of the members. The chairperson, after hearing the feelings of each member (after a reasonable period for questions and discussion), should try to sum up the sense of the commission and prod the members to produce a motion capturing it. The commission should also be spurred into taking action promptly enough to be considered decisive, so that items held over and over do not contaminate and ultimately paralyze action on new business.

A leading reason for planning commission bog-downs is the tendency of some of the members to become amateur experts and try to pass on technical details beyond a layman's ability to judge.

Fred Bair advised:

One thing planning commissions should not be expected to do any longer than it takes to get a competent professional staff, is render amateur judgments on relatively complex technical matters. Policy, yes; determinations as to whether drainage for a forty-acre subdivision is adequate, no. If regulations are well drawn and if the planning staff has the necessary technical ability or knows where to find out, if it doesn't, the less the planning commission goes into details, the better. One obvious obstacle to planning action in many cities and counties is the tendency to make big ones out of little ones to the point where we can't find time to deal properly with really large issues.[3]

4. **The commission wastes people's time.** Don't ever make people who've come for a 7:30 hearing wait hours to be heard or, worse yet, make them come back again because there wasn't time. Insist on the staff estimating and scheduling an adequate time for hearing controversial items in making up an agenda. Take up routine items and unopposed items first and let the people connected with them go home. Stick to the

[3] Bair, *Planning Cities.*

schedule listed on the agenda. Since the commission usually has the time to make decisions after the passions of a public hearing, don't fear holding the commission discussion over until the next meeting. This practice will also help move things along expeditiously on the agenda. Finally, make sure the agenda for any single meeting isn't overloaded. Schedule an extra meeting now and then to clear any backlog of items that need to be considered. This is better than trying to make everyone stay up until the wee hours of the morning to watch the commission heroically fight off sleep as it tries to finish an overlong list of agenda items.

Some further public meeting do's and don't's are the following:

☐ During a hearing, allow people holding the floor to direct questions through the chairperson to anyone they wish, if the answers to the questions will develop factual information that will be of assistance to the commission in reaching a decision. Do not allow anyone to play "Perry Mason" and cross-examine someone to establish his good or bad character or to shake his previous testimony. Commissions do not have to follow the formalities of a court of law (usually they do not swear in witnesses, nor are they bound by the rules of evidence as to what may or may not be introduced as testimony). Attorneys for proponents or opponents often try to tie commissions into procedural knots by trying to get them to adopt the high protocol of a murder trial in the court. Don't be stampeded, especially by attorneys who have clients whose interests are being treated by the commission. When in doubt as to how to proceed, the commission should recess for an opinion from its own lawyer. *Don't act on legal advice by anyone else's lawyer.*

☐ The products of a good hearing from the commission's and the public's viewpoint are answers to the following:

a. Did it define the issues upon which a decision has to be made?

b. Did the evidence provide enough of the conceptual factual basis for reaching a decision?

c. How does the proposal match the existing comprehensive plan and land-use controls? If not, was a sound reason for deviating from them established in the testimony?

☐ If there were experts (planners, real estate appraisers, traffic engineers) produced by either side, the commission should not be afraid to make certain that the expert is not just handing out superficial opinions and glittering generalities. If the commission comes to the meeting knowing what information it has to get at the hearing, then it can dig behind the generalities for the facts it needs. Remember, the hired expert is paid to persuade, not inform. The commission should try to establish whether the "expert" testimony is worthwhile by testing the expert, as follows:

a. What precisely are the expert's qualifications?

b. Before he decided that what his client wants to do is the best way to do something, had the expert considered alternatives? If so, what, and why weren't they as good as the one he advocates?

c. Test the expert with the commission's own local knowledge. Ask, for example, whether he knows the nature of the public services in and around the area he's telling the commission about. Test whether he's been on the property and become familiar with what he's being expert about; you can do this by asking him to describe the land conditions, drainage, water supply, or traffic access to the property. If the meeting produces a property evaluation expert, he'll probably say that the property is practically worthless as presently zoned and that the highest and best use[4] is what's being requested by his client. Ask for comparable sales and why they are comparable, to establish if there's been a real appraisal or he's giving his personal opinion (for a price).

d. Take information from each speaker at a meeting. Keeping notes is a good way. Skim off the rhetoric and put down the facts. Do those facts pertain to what the commission has to decide? Watch out for issues that are diversions from the main responsibility of a commission in a matter. For example, a developer may ask for higher density on the grounds that his dwelling units will be for childless families only. This may be immaterial if the local ordinances deal only with the number of units per acre rather than the number of bedrooms or the kind of purchasers or renters permitted.

☐ Sometimes the commission may not have enough information to make a proper decision on a proposal. In such cases, the

---

92   [4] "Highest and best use" is a real estate term that ought not to be given much currency when the public interest is the prime consideration (see Chapter 2).

commission should say something like: "We don't know whether this is the proper place for this development until we have a plan for the area, a survey, a study, or a report that will give us the information upon which a decision can be based." One test of whether more information is needed would be: Is the commission able to make a decision about a proposal on the basis of what should happen in the area rather than merely whether the proposal itself is intrinsically good or bad? Even a good development in an adverse environment will produce negative results.

☐ Many times, it's as important to be *not* misunderstood as it is to be understood. For example, numerous hearings have attracted an angry crowd of people who had seen renderings of buildings or gradings they didn't like, when all the commission could rule on was whether or not the zone should be changed. Further hearings would be necessary to hammer out site plans and architectural details, but the notices were inadequate, the crowd came down to protest something it had misunderstood and the meeting became an angry farce. If some possibility of public misunderstanding exists, notices should clearly state what will be considered at the meeting and what will not. Then, at the meeting, the chairperson should announce exactly what's at issue and that if rezoned, the way will not be open to have those buildings built. There will be another hearing and all will have a fair chance to give testimony on that subject then.

A Note of Caution:

Even the most well-organized commission will be criticized for doing a poor job of planning. This is largely because within the limitations commissioners work under, they can only do part of what needs to be done for the cities and counties of America. A veteran planning commissioner described the situation as follows:

What is the reality of planning in most American cities? City government has the least power of any governmental level to make the really critical decisions about the lives of citizens, but they must in fact meet the day-to-day needs. City government has the least amount of funds available, particularly general funds for real discretionary use. What funds it has usually come from regressive tax sources—worst of all, property taxes which force it into parochial land-use decisions, often not in the regional interest, which often "beggar its neighbor" and distort policies into "serving" the tax base.

*Because most land is privately owned and the public sector is impoverished, commissions spend most of their time putting out fires in the area of control over private aggrandizement in land use or in land divisions for private development which will not meet identified public needs. If the commission understands the pressures for bad development, they may devise restrictive ordinances which can generally **prevent** things from happening but have no motive power whatsoever to make what **is** desired and in the public interest happen. The lack of public funds to . . . publicly provide for citizens' needs, rather than hope private enterprise will, makes the job of a planning commissioner pretty discouraging.*[5]

While this lament is generally true enough to be almost universal, the possibilities for doing a better job have been enlarged in a number of ways, such as legislation in many states strengthening local planning powers (e.g., Environmental Impact Reports, greater control over subdivisions and lot splits, extraterritorial zoning powers), court decisions enhancing the powers of commissions to implement and enforce plans and ordinances, and greater interest in good planning by the various states and federal government through revenue sharing, direct aid to open space and agricultural preservation programs, and coordinated land-use and transportation policy (e.g., increased aid to transit). While land-use controls are one of the few powers local governments retain, they have been stretched to cover everything from the control of sex shows to the provision of affordable housing through an imaginative technique called "inclusionary zoning."[6] This is one of the public benefits of having many small governments approaching problems from many different directions, just as many research labs effectively converge on the solution to a scientific problem.

---

[5] Quoted from a letter by Dorothy Walker, planning commissioner, Berkeley, California.

[6] " 'Inclusionary housing' or 'inclusionary zoning' is a technique whereby the political subdivision . . . simply mandates that for every X number of units of conventional housing a developer wants to build, a certain percentage must be in the 'affordable range' (e.g., 80–120 percent of the local median income). In return the developer gets bonus density provisions (permission to build more units per acre than the present zoning allows) and a number of other incentives. . . ." From Don G. Campbell, "Zoning Tries to Cure High House Prices," in *Portland Oregonian*, August 7, 1980, p. A24.

Due Process or How to Be Fair

7

*. . . Members of commissions with the role of conducting fair
and impartial fact-finding hearings must, as far as practicable,
be open minded, objective, impartial, free of entangling
influences, and capable of hearing the weak voices as well as
the strong.*

—Supreme Court of Washington
Buell v. *City of Bremerton* (1972)

The courts have said very clearly that local governments'
decisions in planning and zoning don't have to be wise but
they do have to be fair. The legal term for fairness in such
decision making is "due process." Substantive due process
involves using legislative powers so that no one is deprived of
their rights or property. Inverse condemnation is one example
of an abuse of this kind of due process. The important thing
here is to find the correct middle ground between the use of
the police power for the public welfare and proper respect for
the rights of the individual and his or her private property. How
far regulations can go is constantly being redetermined by the
courts and the circumstances of the times.

Procedural due process is probably the area where most
commissions have more of their problems. The rules of fair
play in this kind of due process are as follows:

1. **Adequate notice:** When a matter is going to have a public
   hearing, interested or potentially interested parties should
   receive notice far enough in advance to study what is involved
   and think about what their response is going to be.

   While many state statutes and local ordinances cover the
   details of noticing for hearings, they are often only legal

95

minimums and not really designed to achieve communication. Requirements, for example, that "notice be given in a newspaper in general circulation in the area" often means a block of tiny type buried in the classifieds of a newspaper many citizens don't even subscribe to, much less read. Posting a notice on or in front of the property and/or mailing to property owners and neighborhood associations in the vicinity works much better in terms of communicating. The notices should announce the time and place of the hearing, a description of the matter to be heard (in clear, nontechnical language), and the extent and location of the property to be considered. A small map showing the property in relation to nearby streets or landmarks is generally very helpful. Planning commission budgets and application fees should provide enough money for adequate clerical help, printing, and mailing of notices.

In highly controversial cases or hearings initiated by the planning commission itself, more notice than usual is advisable. Notices to area-wide groups and organizations, renters as well as owners, etc., should be sent in order to make knowledge of the hearing as open and widespread as possible. In larger jurisdictions, newspapers, radio, and TV can be enlisted to help spread the word about what's being considered at the forthcoming hearing. Without adequate notice, the issue being considered is very often misunderstood and, by the time the hearing is opened, the commission may be gazing out over hundreds of angry and confused citizens.

In one instance, half of the city turned out to decry the architectural monstrosities being proposed by an applicant, as illustrated by some sketches that had been published in the local paper. In truth, the only matter the commission could consider and act on was a change of zone from multiple to commercial; the "architectural sketches" were submitted by the applicant merely to support his contention that he could bring good things to the city if only he had approval of the change in zoning.

In cases of public confusion over what's being decided, the citizens will often exhibit an "off with their heads" attitude toward the applicant, the commission, the staff, and anyone else connected with the proposal. As one irate homeowner told the commission holding the hearing described above, "I don't care if this hearing is only zoning or not, a man who thinks of bringing buildings like the ones in the paper to our town ought to get turned down and turned out!"

2. **Advance disclosure:** Exhibits and studies prepared for the hearing ought to be available for study well in advance of the hearing at some convenient place such as a public library. The staff reports should also be available for public study before the hearing. Some staff planners are against having their recommendations known before the hearing, but since the product of their work is mostly informational it ought to have the widest distribution before the hearing. Attorneys, who would like the quasi-judicial proceedings of planning commissions to resemble those of a courtroom, have urged that applicants be required to provide a list of the people who will testify and a summary of what they will say. Thus there would be advance notice of the testimony of Tom Turgid, the traffic expert, on how the project would not congest the streets. The attorney for the other side might then be able to run out and hire Cuthbert Cartwheel, another traffic expert, to testify to the contrary.

The benefits of a battle of "experts" with respect to clear decision making by a lay commission would probably be dubious and, where environmental impact reports are required, their testimony might also be redundant. However, if both sides could supply a list of which "experts" will testify and a summary of what they'll say, then a more evenhanded advance disclosure could be achieved by letting each side prepare its brief with some knowledge of their opposition's assertions. Conceivably, if these expert analyses were to be based on fact rather than "paid judgments," the commissions' deliberations could benefit from a more searching analysis of the pros and cons of a proposal than if only one side has technical expertise to bring to bear on an issue.

3. **The opportunity to be heard:** This is the major and most sensitive element of due process. It is essential that the chairperson have the skill to make everyone feel they have had their say, while at the same time maintaining control of the meeting and moving it along to a conclusion. The local citizenry can be made to feel that the hearing process is totally unfair if space and time are inappropriate, or the commission denies them the chance to comment on the matter being heard. When the regular hearing place is too small to contain the large number of people expected, then another place for the hearing needs to be found. Public interest should be

estimated before the notices are sent and a school auditorium, church meeting room, or some other place big enough for people to both be heard and hear others should be procured if necessary.

Sometimes an unexpected number of people will arrive for a hearing and jam the hearing room or even overflow into the halls and out of doors. When that happens, the matter should be put over until a more suitable place is found. The chairperson should also have the commission secretary get the names of those who showed up to testify and make sure that they get notice of the new hearing.

4. **Full disclosure:** People interested in a matter being heard by a commission should have an opportunity to see, hear, and examine all of the statements and evidence considered by the commission. This includes any staff reports, plans, studies, pictures, drawings, and surveys presented to the commission as evidence on the rightness or wrongness of the proposal it must decide upon.

Reports of what the commission saw, did, and said on field trips connected with the application should be read into the minutes of the hearing before it is opened for testimony. The courts have tended to be very firm about commission contacts and behavior outside the hearing room. In one case (*No Oil* v. *City of Los Angeles*) a commissioner's off-the-cuff remark on a field trip invalidated a decision by the commission because it was a finding not reported and recorded. Oregon judges[1] have prohibited all *ex parte* contacts for planning commissioners. (*Ex parte* literally means off in a corner where others cannot hear.)

While the laws of due process differ from state to state and even among various cities and counties, the following commonsense guidelines ought to be observed to keep the ugly issue of "secret dealings" from rearing its head:

[1] *Fasano* v. *Board of County Commissioners of Washington County* (1973). Some attorneys in other states take a more liberal attitude about discussions between commissioners and interested parties outside the hearing room. See your city or county attorney and let him make the decision if you are in doubt. The advice here has been culled from the work done by Marlin Smith, a noted Chicago attorney, who has made a study of due process in American land-use regulation proceedings for the Ford Foundation and American Bar Association.

a. If a citizen or applicant calls your home or office to discuss a matter before the commission, refuse firmly and invite this testimony to be given at the hearing so it can be heard out in the open. This includes calls from elected officials.

b. Never go on ad hoc field trips with an applicant or opponents alone or even in pairs. It is best to announce the time and place of such field trips at a commission meeting where they are recorded in the minutes. The press and other interested parties should be invited to come. It is best if the whole commission can make these field trips with staff as a body but, failing this, at least three members should go as a subcommittee designated by the chairperson.

c. All travel costs and food should be at public expense. Trips and entertainment for commissioners paid for by people who would like a favorable decision look like payola and should be prohibited by the commission's own bylaws or rules of procedure.

5. **An opportunity to question the statements and evidence presented by both sides:** Since expert testimony and studies often favor the client's case, questions from both the commission and interested parties should be permitted to bring out all the information such witnesses may have. When questioning of people on one side of an issue is conducted by attorneys or others from the opposing side, all questioning should be through the chair. The chairperson, in turn, should see that the questions are proper to the purpose of bringing out more information on the application relevant to a commission decision. It is important to remember that the commissioners are not sitting as judges in a court of law. Therefore attorneys who attempt to engage in the kind of tooth and fang behavior that is suitable for a murder trial have to be firmly checked by the chairperson, backed by the whole commission. Behavior that is out of place in planning and zoning hearings includes adversary procedures where witnesses testifying are bullied by interruptions, objections of law, and threats of legal action.

Questioning of witnesses that attempts to impair their testimony by pressure tactics is acceptable in a court of law, where a judge and opposing counsel can keep the questioning within bounds. But at a public hearing before a lay commission, it is highly improper and unfair to both the victims and the commission that has a hard enough time evaluating the raw evidence without the added burden of trial lawyer manipulations.

A guideline to keep in mind during such hearings is: The commission is not trying to find out if anyone is guilty or at fault in this matter. It is simply receiving information about the best way to regulate a certain proposal in line with what is best for the community. It is not a murder case jury and so the decision does not have to be without a shadow of a doubt but simply the best judgment in light of not only the evidence, but the plans and policies that have been adopted to guide the decisions.

One of the aims of good planning is to avoid the waste and blight that characterized the commercial overzoning of the past. Land should be designated commercial or industrial in accordance with foreseeable public needs, not speculative ambitions.

6. **Findings of fact backing up decisions:** The decisions themselves are central to the practice of due process. Some rules that several attorneys have recommended are:

   a. The commission should act on the evidence received in as fair and impartial a way as possible. In one California court case, the judge found that the city had made a decision "taking" a man's property and had to pay him $2,000,000 for it, not because their zoning ordinance or general plan was defective, but because the city council people and commissioners had publicly demonstrated such prejudice against the man that he did not first need to seek relief against the restrictive zoning by applying for a change. The judge implied that, on the evidence, this man could not get a fair hearing in that city and that therefore the city had made a taking of his property by restricting him to a business use that was economically unfeasible.

   b. Decisions need to be in written form when they are transmitted to the legislative body. Minutes of the meeting are usually acceptable if they are sufficiently broad in scope. The action a commission takes should be based on specific reasons relating to the zoning ordinance or the general plan that can be detailed in the record. (This includes staff reports as well.) When litigation is probable, a court stenographer is advisable.

   c. Specific factual findings in support of a decision are essential, particularly in granting or denying variances, permits, or plans for subdivisions or planned unit developments. In a 1974 case (*Topanga Association* v. *County of Los Angeles*) the court said: ". . . the agency which renders the challenged decision must set forth findings to bridge the analytic gap between the raw evidence and ultimate decision of order . . . . A findings requirement serves to conduce the administrative body to draw legally relevant sub-conclusions supportive of its ultimate decision: The intended effect is to facilitate orderly analysis and minimize the likelihood that the agency will randomly leap from evidence to conclusions."

What decisions like *Topanga* mean is that ordinances for variances that have criteria requiring a finding "that strict adherence to the zoning ordinance would impose an unnecessary hardship" can't be paraphrased into findings that read: "Whereas the zoning ordinance requires that before a variance is granted, there be a finding that where strict adherence to the zoning ordinance would impose an unnecessary hardship and whereas in this case it was found that there would be such a hardship, the variance is granted." Such a statement is not a finding or the "legally relevant sub-conclusions" called for in *Topanga*, but an unsupported final conclusion.

Other favorite phrases mis-used as findings are: "This change of zone would be consistent with the general plan." "To bring the property as it exists into compliance with the zoning and/or building codes would impose a hardship on the owner." (Often the hardship is self-induced.) "The applicant has demonstrated that the highest and best use of the property is the project proposed and therefore the change of zone is consistent with the economic goals of the general plan which state that the city should try to improve its fiscal position."

Another frequent mistake regarding findings is committed by the lazy commission that votes on something and then asks the staff to supply the reasons. The power of a planning commission springs from the legal requirement that its advice be sought, even if it is not followed. In a situation where a commission jumps from hearing testimony to an action whose supporting findings are to prepared by a staff person, the advice it sends up is valueless to the people advised. Staff people can certainly help, but it is really the job of the commission or commission majority to develop and articulate the logic supporting their actions. This is the basis for having a commission whose major function is advisory. Therefore it is usually more important for a commission to transmit its reasoning on an issue than its vote.

See Appendix F for an example of the kind of report that should follow a quasi-judicial action by a commission or a zoning administrator. Note that this report makes a clear record of all the facts on which a decision was based, and its findings and recommendations are clearly based on facts, relevant regulations, and local policies, so that when the matter is reheard the "analytic gap" between raw evidence and the decision is properly bridged.

7. **Avoid the appearance of impropriety:** Currently there appears to be less trust in government than ever before. Commissioners who have business or financial interests that would stand to profit from a decision obviously ought not participate in the decision making and should absent themselves from the entire hearing so that there be no opportunity for them to appear to influence their colleagues on the commission. When someone is in a business that frequently has interests in applications before the commission, then that person is a dubious choice for the job of planning commissioner. This is because the commission will be weakened by his frequent absences from deliberations if he does step down when there are apparent conflicts of interest or the commission's decisions will be damaged in the public eye if he doesn't. It does not matter that the intent of such a commissioner is to serve fairly and honestly; it is the effect that he has on the commission's reputation and credibility as an objective untainted body that counts.[2]

The courts have shown their displeasure over biased and improper conduct on many occasions, but perhaps most

[2] The Washington Supreme Court commented on this need for public confidence as follows: "The appearance of fairness doctrine has received recent emphasis in our decisions regarding zoning. Basic to this is our recognition that restrictions on the free and unhampered use of property imposed by planning and zoning compel the highest public confidence in governmental processes bringing about such action. Members of commissions with the role of conducting fair and impartial fact-finding hearings must, as far as practicable, be open-minded, objective, impartial, free of entangling influences and capable of hearing the weak voices as well as the strong. The importance of the appearance of fairness has resulted in the recognition that it is necessary only to show an interest which might have influenced a member of the commission and not that it actually so affected him." Buell v. City of Bremerton (1972).

clearly in the case of Washington State's *Smith* v. *Skaget County* (1969). The court said:

The right to be heard implies a reasonable hope of being heeded. The right to be heard in a public hearing contemplates that, although the legislative body may, in finally deciding the matter, draw upon all kinds and sources of information including the opinions of experts, the hearing must be conducted as to be free from bias and prejudice; it must not only be open-minded and fair, but **must have the appearance of being so.** *When the planning commission announced . . . it would go into executive session, it was within its rights. But when, pursuant to this announcement of a closed session, it invited representatives of the aluminum company and other powerful advocates of the zoning changes to attend and be heard, but deliberately excluded opponents of the proposed rezoning, the hearing lost one of its most basic requisites—* **the appearance of elemental fairness.**

The courts may order commissions to preserve the appearance of elemental fairness, but it is better if this fairness is part of a commission's internal structure. In addition to the rules and regulations (see Appendix A) for the commission's operation, there should be a clearly understood code of conduct for the commissioners as individuals and the commission as a whole. Here are some guidelines that should help.

a. Avoid public challenges on conflict of interest charges by heading them off in advance.

b. Gifts of cash, liquor, company products, or anything that has a retail value of $1.98 should be either declined or returned to the sender. Commissioners should also avoid applicant-paid junkets and entertainment.

c. Don't string people along. Make decisions promptly. If a plan or proposal is to be modified before it will be approved, the commission has a moral obligation to be specific about what it wants to look at next time, so that there won't have to be a time after that and another after that, ad infinitum. If the basis for making a decision is lacking—e.g., the area's not planned yet, the appropriate ordinances need to be drawn up first—deny the application without prejudice, rather than trying to play things by ear and stringing the trapped applicant along. Sometimes the applicant is deliberately stalled by official nitpicking, and if the delay and expense he or she is put through by an indecisive commission are not yet illegal everywhere, they ought to be.

d. When should a commissioner resign? All commissioners have some ideas about what their participation in a commission should bring about both for the community and for their own sense of well-being. If not, why would anyone serve in an unpaid job involving long hours, hard work, and lots of pressure? If conditions are such that realization of one's goals becomes remote, a resignation may very well be the best move. If, for example, there is a wide gap between a commissioner's sense of decency and the policies of the council, then it may be in everyone's best interest if he resigned. He's obviously no longer a "trusted advisor." He should not only resign but should do so with a shrill blast of whistleblowing about the neglect of the community's future. His energies might thereafter be best directed to turning the rascals out at the next election.

The "quit line" that must be drawn is in a different location for each individual, but every commissioner should mentally draw one and know early in the term that it lies at the limits of where his or her conscience will go. The line should become sharper the more one is pushed toward it. When the limit is being approached, it may help to give clear warning to those that can do something about the situation that unless specific changes are made, there will be one less commissioner on board. Be prepared to carry out this warning before giving it. Do not be swayed, manipulated, or pressured into backing down from closely held convictions. Nobody should "own" a planning commissioner. A commissioner is nonfunctional if not independent, objective, and operating from his or her own set of convictions.

Nuts and Bolts:
Zoning and Development Review

8

*I have talked about planning as a practical operation, geared
to the daily workings of local government. It is also . . . the key
to sound long-range development of our cities. But unless
and until planning goes to work today, plans for tomorrow
aren't likely to do much good.*

—Fred Bair

*Don't put no constrictions on da people.
Leave them ta hell alone.*

—Jimmy Durante

Why is land use regulated? It has become popular lately to
decry planning and the regulations that implement it as
bureaucratic evils responsible for everything from the high
cost of housing to the decline of American cities. Actually the
country had a lot of experience with unplanned and
unregulated growth just after World War II, when returning
servicemen and newly affluent war workers created the
impetus for what was then termed "the exploding metropolis,"
"the sprawling suburbs," etc. No place in the nation boasted
unrestrained growth more than Los Angeles, which was in
those halcyon days a relative stranger to regulation as well as
to smog, sprawl, and spiraling crime statistics. Remi Nadeau
in 1961 described what happened in the San Fernando Valley
to those free and easy days that many would like to return to by
forgetting what we've learned from them.

*Nowhere was Southern California's growth more spectacular
than in the San Fernando Valley, which was chiefly
responsible for the growth of the city of Los Angeles from 1.5
million just before the war to 2.5 million by [1960]. As late as
1944, about 170,000 people lived in an area the size of
Chicago. . . .*

By 1946 the tract home craze was fairly launched. In the longest uninterrupted real estate boom in the city's history, San Fernando Valley's population multiplied five times to 850,000.

Such an overwhelming inpouring of people was bound to create shortages.

The telephone company found itself more than a year behind in filling orders for new subscribers. The valley's sewer lines were so overloaded that many developers in the west end were forced to use cesspools; for a time, in one section where the earth was unsuited for cesspools, the effluent ran down the streets. By 1953 some 38,000 school children were on half day sessions due to the classroom shortage – most of them in the San Fernando Valley. Evidence of overcrowding was everywhere. Ex G.I.'s who had vowed never to stand in line again found themselves queuing up for everything from the grocery counter to the parking lot. . . .

The valley's worst single difficulty is its inadequate street system; except for the widening of a few arteries, it is substantially the same as it was before the war. In essence a community the size of San Francisco is trying to make out with country roads. . . . Only two arteries lead out of this vast area to the industrial centers of Los Angeles and these are jammed bumper to bumper. Public transportation is wholly inadequate. . . .[1]

The tragedy that befell the San Fernando Valley is a classic case of what happens when a boom bursts upon an unprepared area. Like many booming areas today, the local authorities simply would not or could not match the rate of growth with their capacities to provide vital services and facilities. When advance planning has not taken place to ensure a balance between new development and local resources to provide for it and a good fit with the natural and manmade environment of the place, then the development is not only unplanned but also unregulated, in the sense that to regulate is to reduce to order. Where there is no organized foresight (a good definition of planning), regulation usually becomes an empty formality.

[1] Remi Nadeau, *Los Angeles from Mission to Modern City* (New York: Longmans Green & Co., 1961), pp. 275–279.

With this caveat in mind, let's turn to the activity on which a commission spends a majority of its time — processing development proposals and applications.

The following are **the four major functions of a planning commission in development review:**

a. Acting as an arbiter among the planning staff, the applicants, and other interested parties (citizens, property owners, other governmental units, etc.). In addition, the commission must have the ability to resolve differences among its own members sufficiently to send well-reasoned and clear recommendations to the legislative body.

b. Carrying out the development review process within the legal framework and requirements of a complex body of law, especially when they sit as a quasi-judicial body applying the rules and regulations to an application. While the courts have been very reluctant to substitute their judgment for that of a local planning agency, they have been quick to pounce on errors, omissions, and violations of correct procedure. For example, judges have been very ready to strike down the actions of jurisdictions that did not have an Environmental Impact Report that was "adequate" (i.e., considered everything). In one California case, the approval of a motel was set aside because the county did not have an EIR that considered the impact of the specifically lower number of units suggested by the opposition.

c. Reviewing the project in view of the standards and technical criteria which constitute the developmental review criteria (site conditions, traffic, design, impacts, plan conformity, etc.). Since this often involves highly technical battles between experts, lay commissioners often get snowed under with technical jargon and complexity.

It is therefore very important for commissioners to understand how to work from their strengths and avoid becoming exploited techno-peasants.[2] For example, if an applicant is offering experts in marketing, soils, architecture, real estate appraisal, traffic engineering, motivational psychology, and

[2] A "techno-peasant" is someone whose future is in the hands of technocrats. Good techno-peasants may not know how things work, but because they are so commonsensical, they insist on knowing what technical things mean. (From Katha Pollitt in *Next,* March/April 1981.)

law to contend that the merits of a project are so exceptional that all approvals should be granted this very night, it might well be, as it often is, that the real issue is a land-use question—namely, should a forty-two-story high-rise condominium be permitted as a planned unit development in the midst of the city's most desirable single-family neighborhood. However, many developers still choose to "sell the project" when the land-use issues are dubious. It's the commission's job not only to have the issue defined but also to stick to it. Overly technical issues are best delegated to staff (or objective consultants if staff can't handle it), rather than having the commission sit up half the night trying to determine whether the drain pipes are large enough or the proposed steeply cut embankment will hold in very wet weather.

d. Dealing with the local political environment. As John Dyckman said, "Planning is *in* politics and cannot escape politics, but it is not politics. . . . Every land-use decision, every transportation decision, every economic strategy has a political content in the sense that the distribution of benefits and costs of that action falls unequally on people. We can have no illusions about our work in that regard."[3]

On the other hand, many of the planners dream of a tech-fix for all problems. As George Sternlieb put it, "Now my own definition of the planning role is that planners provide the numbers. It is the politicians who must determine the definition of virtue."[4] Commissioners cannot escape into the illusion that all costs and benefits can be quantified, verified, and sanctified by the production of numbers. First of all, politicians tend to embrace numbers only when they agree with the conclusions. They are much more likely to count costs and benefits in terms of friends (votes, contributions, support) and strangers (people without the clout to affect their political future). Planning commissions were originally conceived of as a means of keeping planning out of politics. A more realistic view is that commissions should be a halfway house between the numbers-makers and the politicians so that planning is

[3] John W. Dyckman, "Three Crises of American Planning," in *Planning Theory in the 1980's,* Robert W. Burchell and George Sternlieb, eds. (New Brunswick, N.J.: Rutgers University, The Center for Urban Policy Research, 1978).

[4] George Sternlieb, "Seven Hills on the Way to the Mountain: The Role of Planning and the Planners," in *Planning Theory in the 1980's.*

neither wholly numbers nor wholly politics. To do this, commissioners need to develop an outlook that understands both approaches but is uniquely their own — for example, a set of values about what is suitable for their kind of community and its aspirations. This may well mean resisting a development that will provide the kind of short-range gains that politicians find hard to resist or one that checks out by the numbers but really doesn't fit in. In my town, it was a standard Taco Bell Restaurant facing the Civic Center.

An overview of zoning: Zoning came first and is the uniquely American way of handling land use. The basic idea was to zone land into districts where all the users that were compatible would share the same designation. Thereafter they could build as a matter of right, provided they built within the prescribed envelope and met some minimal standards of height, off-street parking, and other guidelines.

Zoning's basic purposes are:

a. To maintain property values (and the local tax base) on the theory central to planning that values are preserved and enhanced by orderly as opposed to haphazard growth.

b. To stabilize and maintain the character of neighborhoods (and business districts).

c. To provide for uniform regulations throughout each district. While this aspect has allowed monotony and is why planned unit development is controversial, it supports predictability from the standpoint of demands on public services and facilities.

d. To move traffic rapidly and safely. Street widths are keyed to zoning, and off-street parking requirements are justified on the basis of maintaining street capacity and public safety. The introduction of higher density or nonresidential uses in single-family neighborhoods is often effectively opposed because of increased traffic generation, which will be a danger to children and peace and quiet in the home, as well as the contention that curbside parking[5] will disappear and traffic jams and accidents will proliferate.

---

[5] Some cities regulate curbside parking by nonresidents by issuing stickers to residents and prohibiting parking by others (e.g., San Francisco and Portland, Oregon).

e. To regulate competition. As one southwestern wag put it, "We're just a small city and one shopping center will serve most of our needs. Two will just barely survive, while three would be ruinously competitive, and four will make us like Phoenix"!

f. To control nuisances and maintain architectural standards. Courts have upheld jurisdictions that deny permits for structures so at variance with existing structures as to cause a depreciation of property values. One city (*Oregon City* v. *Harthe*) was upheld in banning junkyards for aesthetic reasons.

Over the years it was found that some uses didn't fit into zoning categories and districts. Many had a high nuisance potential, like glue works, tanneries, and pet hospitals, or were socially dubious, like trailer parks and massage parlors. So the *special use permit* was devised to allow the community to look over and modify, exclude, or so restrict as to deny uses that might raise problems.

As the need for greater flexibility grew because of the arrival of complex and large-scale projects such as regional shopping centers, planned communities of hundreds of homes, industrial parks, and hotel-convention centers, regulation turned to controls based on the regulation of the project itself.

One early example is the *floating zone.* This kind of zone is described in a zoning ordinance but is not given a place on the zoning map. If the right project in the right place were submitted, then the floating zone would descend to earth anchored by conditions not listed in the regular zoning ordinance.

Some jurisdictions went so far as to use *contract zoning,* a procedure whereby conditions running with the land are attached to an approval of a certain use. These conditions were not found in the regular zoning ordinance, and if the applicant were to sell property to a third party, it would be subject to the covenants agreed to by the local government and the applicant. Planned unit development ordinances brought development review almost fully into the arena of negotiation and out of regulation by fixed standards and ordinance language. Thus many planned unit development provisions supplant both the existing subdivisions and zoning ordinances that allow development without reference to lot sizes, density limits, mixing of uses, and types of dwelling unit normally prohibited. The developments are approved on their merits such as good design, benefits to the community, public need for the project, preservation of environmental values (e.g., preservation of scenic areas, habitats, views, open spaces, etc.), and social benefits such as provision of moderate-income housing.

Handling zone applications: Mr. Justice Sutherland, in the definitive *Village of Euclid (Ohio)* v. *Ambler Realty* case, laid the legal foundation for zoning in his comment, "Each community has the right and responsibility to determine its own character and as long as that determination did not disturb the orderly growth of the region and nation, it was a valid use of the police power."[6]

Zoning is the single activity that takes up most of a commission's time in a majority of cities and counties. More citizens come in contact with zoning, either as applicants, protesters, or simply observers of the incessant boundary wars that heat up commission chambers week after week, than with any other aspect of the commission's work. Yet the cliché that "planning isn't zoning" still has wide currency. Planning is held to be an arcane intellectual ritual where a group of people peer into the future with the assistance of a technical shaman until they can finish the sentence, "Wouldn't it be nice if ---" with enough hopeful words to fill a fairly thick report. Zoning, on the other hand, according to believers in this myth, is supposed to be merely a local legal code like the building, penal, electrical, plumbing, business, and licensing codes—namely, a list of rules on what you can or can't do with your property, except that a smart lawyer can usually bend these rules in his client's favor.

So why do we make such a fuss over zoning? There are many critics of zoning's shortcomings and some have suggested drastic overhauls or doing away with it entirely. Professor John Reps singled out the following major ones:

[6] Another interpretation of this statement is that a jurisdiction is obligated to relate its land-use controls to the orderly growth of the areas outside its boundaries. This interpretation may have an important bearing on court tests of local growth-limitation ordinances.

a. Zoning regulations are intensely parochial. Standards required in any single metropolitan area may vary enormously depending on the whims of local legislators. We make much of the principle that land similarly situated must be similarly zoned within a given municipality, but this concept is cruelly violated when a homogeneous area is zoned for industry on one side of a municipal boundary line and high class low-density residential uses on the other side.

b. We have Balkanized our cities into districts with precise and rigid boundary lines. We have established categories of uses that have segregated rather than integrated functional portions of cities and which have often disregarded the interrelationships between widely separated categories of uses.

c. Ultimate review of zoning regulations and administrative action is a judicial function. Courts are more and more being called on to decide issues which are increasingly technical and complex. Most courts have taken refuge in the doctrine of the presumption of legislative validity, but as the thrust of regulations becomes more vigorous, it is unlikely that courts can refuse to decide issues on their merits. Yet they are ill-equipped to make decisions on technical matters and it is far from clear that the adversary system provides the best approach to decision making.[7]

Others have criticized zoning as being unable to keep up with new innovations. More important, zoning stands accused of not having come through as the prime shaper of new urban growth that early planning theory intended it to be.

Dennis O'Harrow made the following points about why people want to keep zoning controls despite its shortcomings:

The point of current criticism of zoning is not so much that it failed in its original purpose, but that it disappointed those who saw it as the creative force to shape the future city. They protested loudly that zoning was not "planning," but at the same time they tried to use zoning to carry out all of their plans, an assignment it was not equipped to do.

There may be more congestion in the streets today than there was the day the zoning ordinance was adopted, but there is much less congestion than there would have been without the

[7] John Reps, "Requiem for Zoning," in *Taming Metropolis*, Vol. II (New York: Anchor Books, 1967). Used by permission.

zoning ordinance. Zoning has done this by keeping traffic-creating uses out of residential neighborhoods and by putting them along streets better able to carry the traffic they create.

Zoning has also been effective in keeping unwanted uses out of homogeneous neighborhoods, its detractors to the contrary notwithstanding. Those of us who follow the zoning administration in our own city or the zoning decisions in the courts sometimes get the idea that all is Sturm und Drang, the whole structure of zoning is falling to pieces around our ears. Our vision is warped, our hearing is defective. For every "bad" (in our opinion) ruling by the board of adjustment, 500 occupancy permits are authorized routinely and in full compliance with the zoning regulations. For each "bad" (in our opinion) decision by an appellate court, owners of 5,000 to 50,000 single-family homes relax under full zoning protection.

If you want protection for your property—and there is nothing unreasonable in such a desire—what is your alternative to zoning? According to the opponents of zoning, the alternative is the private covenant:

a. *Unless there are deed restrictions on your land **and** on that of all your neighbors within the blighting radius of a drive-in hamburger joint or used car lot or billboard, you cannot expect to start now and get those restrictions written into the deeds.*

b. *If you do a little research on how unreliable most private covenants have been as protective devices, and what costs there would be if you as an individual try to enforce a private covenant, you will understand why land use regulation by your own government is to be preferred.*

The boil and bubble of urban building, and rebuilding, the turmoil caused by population growth, migration, expanding markets, personal affluence, new technology, and a dozen other economic and social forces has knocked a lot of holes in our zoning plans. Those who thought that zoning was forever are disappointed.

But in spite of its battle scars, community zoning is still giving millions of people the assurances they want—assurance that their city will be a place to be proud of, assurance that their neighborhood will be a pleasant, and financially secure, surrounding for their home.

No community without zoning can make the same claim. And so far as we know, there is not a single urban community with

*zoning that would repeal the ordinance and try to get along
without zoning.*[8]

A serious deficiency in many communities' zoning patterns is
that segregation of people, incomes, and home values, in
addition to land uses, is built into the way zoning is applied.
When this is the case, zoning is thought of as a hierarchy of
uses rising up from the lowly industrial and agricultural catch-
all zones up to the sovereign single-family zone. Within the
single-family zones, class differences are preserved in the
form of minimum lot sizes. In one New England town in which
I was employed, 6,000-square-foot lot sizes signified Slavic mill
hands; quarter-acre tracts equalled newlywed white collar
workers; half-acre lots meant upwardly mobile professionals;
one-acre estates formed the "golden ghetto" of Jewish
doctors, dentists, lawyers, and CPAs; two-acre plots
represented the old-line Yankee families and corporate elite at
the crest of local society. The lot sizes were as unmixable as
fire and water. Over the years some inroads have been made
into the suburban caste system in form of planned unit
developments, mobile home parks, and condominium projects
that mix incomes and backgrounds somewhat more.

In many surburbs and smaller towns, however, the public
official who votes for violation of the social barriers that the
zoning boundaries represent is headed for early retirement.
Many believe that these attitudes form a suburban noose
around the older center cities, keeping the poor and racial
minorities penned into their own ghettos.

Constance Perin claims that American land-use regulations
are culturally defined and translate local principles of what the
social order should be into settlement patterns on the land.
Some of the principles of class, status, and power that
homeowners use to pressure commissioners are:

1. Density is inversely proportional to status. Thus the highest
   status is accorded to people having the most remote
   relationships with their neighbors and the lowest to those who
   have the most proximate. This principle is often at the core of
   opposition to PUDs.

114
[8] Dennis O'Harrow, "Zoning: What's the Good of It," in *Taming Metropolis,* Vol.
II. Used by permission.

2. People having blood relationships with those with whom they share a house are more highly valued than those joining together out of friendship or economic necessity.

3. Property values are really home prices in the resale market. Homeowners are thus often small-time real estate speculators who use terms like "high neighborhood standards" to mean homogeneous neighborhoods, so letting in of people of different incomes, races, or even housing type preferences will mean that they will no longer have the kind of location that the next buyer would pay top dollar to move into.

4. Owners are more valued people than renters. Owners have more valuable behavior; among the most important is the fact that they have qualified at a bank and have a credit rating as well as a stake in the community.

5. The suburbs transformed the greatest distance from home to work into the prime symbolic reward for achieving the American dream. However, such high-income suburbs continue to exclude the people who maintain and protect the community (teachers, nurses, fire- and policemen, etc.).

6. Privacy is valued because it is a way of managing and controlling social interactions with neighbors by having enough land and physical boundaries. Not hearing the neighbors and choosing the time you'll see each other are highly prized. Added to this is the widespread belief that high-density living causes stress.

7. In property markets new economic ventures are often valued more highly than those previously established (e.g., new shopping center versus old downtown).[9]

Perin concludes that "Once it's better understood, the judicial question of discriminatory intent versus effect will become obsolete: our culture is intentional."[10] From the conservative

[9] Adapted from Constance Perin, *Everything in Its Place* (Princeton, N.J.: Princeton University Press, © 1977). Used by permission. These points are largely summarized from the more lengthy text of the book.

[10] Ibid. Apparently the Supreme Court of the United States agrees. In the case of *James* v. *Valticara* (1971), the court found that Article 34 of the California State Constitution, which provided that no low-rent housing project could be developed, acquired, or constructed until the project was approved by a majority of those in the local jurisdiction voting in a mandatory referendum, did not discriminate against or deny equal protection to low-income persons, even though the Equal Protection Clause of the Constitution prohibits the states from discriminating between the poor *as such* in the application of their laws.

side, economist Anthony Downs underscores this hypothesis of an intentional dual system by claiming that it does not come as a result of the free market system but by the weight of the affluent majority. He says, "Urban development in America is frequently described as 'chaotic' and 'unplanned.' . . . But economically, politically and socially American urban development occurs in a systematic highly predictable manner. It leads to precisely the results desired by those who dominate it . . . [ghettos and suburbs are] created, sustained, and furthered by public policies and laws that prevent free markets from operating. Those policies and laws are designed to protect the vested interests of the urban majority at a terrible cost to the poor who constitute a relative minority in our society."[11]

However, in an increasing number of areas, it's the majority that is being excluded from housing, especially in hot growth areas. A study of housing demand in the eighties at the University of California, Berkeley, estimated "that by the time the 1990 census comes around the average home will cost more than $220,000." It continues:

The enormous demand for housing will mean some 21 million housing units will be needed over this decade . . . and with price rises continuing but at a slower (12 percent) rate, the cost of today's mythical dwelling will double within 10 years.

Would you have believed anyone who told you that the tract house you moved into after World War II, costing $14,000 then, would be worth $100,000 someday?[12]

Because so much of the potential home-buying public is being frustrated by skyrocketing home prices, local government intervention to secure "affordable housing" is being attempted in such diverse places as Boulder, Colorado;

[11] Anthony Downs, *Opening up the Suburbs* (New Haven, Conn.: Yale University Press, 1973).

[12] Kenneth T. Rosen, *The Demand for Housing Units in the 1980's* (Berkeley, Calif.: Center for Real Estate and Urban Economics, University of California, Berkeley, 1980). Quoted from a story by Dick Turpin in *Portland Oregonian,* December 8, 1980.

Montgomery County, Maryland; and Orange County, California. They are trying a technique known as "inclusionary zoning," whereby the local zoning authority simply says that for every X number of market-priced houses a developer wants to build, a certain percentage must be in the affordable range for middle-income residents.

In Orange County, for example, the aim of the inclusionary zoning scheme is to provide homes for people who have annual incomes (1980) falling in a range from 80 to 120 percent of the overall county median income. This range is $18,400–$27,600, so the developer is required to build about 25 percent of the units to be priced between $46,000 and $69,000 in an area where the median-priced home is $103,000. In return the developer receives density bonuses (permission to build more units per acre than is permitted by present zoning on the property), an acceleration in project processing, and other incentives. (Speed in development processing is a very real cost consideration because with interest rates at 18 percent per year, each month of processing delay adds 1½ percent to the cost of the project—more if inflation in building costs and materials is added in.)

In other areas, including Canada, the housing crises may be tackled by some of the following suggested solutions:

a. Put a sales tax on nonprimary residences (mainly homes bought for investment and speculation) to raise money for first-time-homeowner mortgages.

b. Remove high building standards for owner-occupied housing.

c. Make public land available for cooperative housing even if it's zoned single family.

d. Increase capital gains and real estate transfer taxes for sales of homes that are not primary residences, thus capturing some of the speculators' gains and discouraging the practice in single-family homes.

e. Allow people to build their own houses on a modular basis.

f. Allow mobile homes on single-family lots.

g. Allow add-a-rental or separate second units in single-family zones, particularly where there are large houses, large lots, or both.

Understanding the police powers vested in planning commissions: One of the biggest problems commissions have in doing their job as regulators is understanding the difference between public interests and property rights. Many attorneys, for example, still argue that an owner has the right to do what he wants to do with his property if what he proposes to do doesn't "hurt" his neighbors. However, the right to develop land has increasingly become a privilege rather than a right. The legal argument for this shift is offered by Professor Ira M. Heyman of the University of California, who states:

Private property is in fact a creation of the laws of the land. . . . For seven centuries the English, and later the American, courts in deciding thousands of cases worked out rules and principles of enforced neighborliness. Each cut down on argued "rights" of absolute dominion . . . . Rights in property have been defined and protected by courts only to the extent that such rights and protections are consistent with social, economic, and political realities. How far regulations can go is basically a political question.[13]

Heyman leaves the protection of a property owner's right to dispose of and use his land resting almost entirely upon the vague concept that "regulations must be reasonable as applied to particular parcels of land." He offers four tests of reasonableness that should be applied to governmental restrictions upon private property. They are:

1. *Does the regulation reasonably relate to a proper legislative goal?*

2. *Regulations must not unfairly discriminate against similarly situated property owners . . . . Similarly, courts are often disturbed where a zoning amendment or variance or conditional-use permit is granted which allows the successful applicant to carry on a profitable activity denied to his neighbors under the general zoning regulations . . . . An intelligently prepared general plan with consistent regulation guards against the prohibited type of discrimination. Courts are least likely to find unreasonable differentiating regulations based on the forethought evidenced in a competently prepared plan.*

[13] Ira M. Heyman, "The Great Property Rights Fallacy," *Cry California,* Summer 1968, published by *California Tomorrow,* San Francisco. Used by permission.

3. *A third idea which finds considerable mention in judicial discussions of "reasonableness" is the impact of a regulation on the market value of the land to which it is being applied. A consistent series of California cases indicates that it is constitutionally irrelevant that a contested regulation substantially lowers the potential market value of the objector's parcel, so long as the regulation is otherwise reasonable (i.e., it supports a justified public goal and is not discriminatory) . . . .*

4. *The fourth idea implicit in the notion of reasonableness involves the idea of spreading to the public the costs of acquiring public benefits. The California (and U.S.) Constitution requires the payment of "just compensation" upon the taking or damaging of private property . . . . Regulation, technically, does not involve "taking" or "damaging" property. Nevertheless, courts, on occasion, have struck down regulations on the ground they seek to accomplish purposes for which eminent domain (with payment of compensation) should have been used.*[14]

Generally speaking, zoning should not be used to keep a parcel vacant, but any exaction or dedication closely tied to a public purpose would seem to meet the test of reasonableness if it's uniformly applied. Thus, cities have imposed such requirements as bedroom taxes, open-space dedications, and low-income housing quotas on new developments to offset housing's general inability to pay fully for the services it receives. In supporting an ordinance requiring dedications for street widenings as a prerequisite for an owner getting a building permit, a California court (*Southern Pacific Company v. City of Los Angeles*) found that the forced dedication requirement wasn't unreasonable because it was simply another application of the principle that the exercise of the police power in traffic regulation cases is simply a risk the property owner assumes when he lives in modern society under modern traffic conditions.

When is land-use regulation more than an exercise of the police power? The courts have not been clear on the issue of whether rezoning property to a less intensive use is compensable because of a diminution of land value. In the

---

[14] Ibid. Refer to the definition of inverse condemnation in Chapter 2.

case of *Asartra Ltd. Partnership v. City of Palo Alto* (1975),[15] the Federal District Court found that the city's actions in first attempting to buy a 500-acre property and, failing in that, subsequently denying a residential development permit, followed by a rezoning from residential planned development to open space, really constituted an excessive use of eminent domain power without compensation. The open-space rezoning, according to the Court, actually acquired rights over the property for the enjoyment of the general public without compensation for the potential profit extending from planned development zoning.

In both rezonings and subdivision exactions it's usually difficult to determine when regulation becomes an improper taking. One legislative test is whether the exactions are justified by the compensation the property owner receives from the flow of benefits that come from approval to develop. The degree of diminution of land value is not really applicable if the rezoning is tied to some clear public purpose connected to the use of the police power. Lawyers more frequently rely on invalidating a commission's action on the bases that:

1. It's arbitrary because there *isn't* a rational relationship between the application of the regulation and the legislative purpose of the regulation;

2. It's confiscatory because it deprives the regulated property of all reasonable value, despite the public good achieved; or

3. It's discriminatory because equal treatment is not afforded those equally situated. (This is not applicable to the owner seeking a gas station on the fourth corner of an intersection where three already exist but does apply to the parcel in the middle of a block zoned for apartments that is zoned for single-family use.)

Aesthetic zoning and design review: Despite the oft-repeated cliche that "You can't legislate taste," the law sometimes takes exception. For example, a California legal journal said:

Great expansion in actual accomplishment of aesthetic purposes has occurred in the field of zoning and the related fields of planning and subdivision regulations . . . in practice planning and zoning boards and commissions . . . in dealing

---

[15] What makes this case unclear is that California law did not permit the use of eminent domain for the acquisition of open space.

*with zoning matters commonly consider and give great weight
to aesthetic factors in enacting and administering regulations
of all the various types involved in comprehensive zoning . . . .*

*In general, though such factors have been considered and
though they may have been the moving factor in the enactment
and administration of zoning regulations, it has not been
necessary for the courts to rely on aesthetic purposes to
uphold the zoning action taken. They have been able to base
their decisions on long recognized and well established police
power purposes and have either avoided mention of aesthetic
matters or have coupled them with other purposes in
supporting zoning enactments or decisions.[16]*

Regulation that seeks to protect the aesthetic quality of life
and the human environment was further strengthened by
Justice Douglas of the U.S. Supreme Court in delivering the
court opinion in *Village of Belle Terre* v. *Bruce Borass et al:*
"The police power is not confined to elimination of filth, stench
and unhealthy places. It is ample to lay out zones where family
values, youth values and the blessings of quiet seclusion and
clear air make the area a sanctuary for people."

Some Basic Hints for Better Zoning

A. **Periodically review and update the zoning ordinance.** For
example, many towns had commercial zone requirements that
were designed for the old downtown center or strip
commercial developments. When the integrated shopping
center mixed offices, stores, and sometimes even residences
on a large single site, the local ordinances were entirely
inadequate for handling the parking, design, sign control,
height, and land-use problems presented by the new kind of
commercial center. The same situation pertained in many
jurisdictions when the boom in mobile home parks erupted
(their ordinances were for travel trailer camps to be used by
transient tourists and migratory workers). When the recent
spurt in townhouse and condominium apartments occurred,
many local ordinances had regulations only for rental
apartment units. More recently, there have been problems with
the conversion of older rental apartment buildings to
individually owned condominium units.

[16] 55 *Cal Jurisprudence* 2d S86.

B. **Control creeping change with buffer zones between residential zones and those uses which have the kind of adverse effects on residential zones that lead to endless requests for changes of zoning boundaries.** These requests often come from the single-family lots next to the noisy apartments, busy stores, and oily filling stations on busy thoroughfares. The owners come to the planning commission to ask for relief through a change of zone so that they can replace the now useless or uninhabitable house with a similar noisy apartment, busy store, or oily filling station. A buffer zone should stabilize the situation by permitting uses such as professional offices, clinics, small churches, and mortuaries, which are more compatible neighbors to the homes on the street and also a transitional use between the intensive uses and the housing areas. Buffer zone building standards (height, bulk, signs, design) should definitely be compatible with the homes.

The trend in planning has been moving more to the use's "performance" (noise, traffic generation, smoke, visual, and other impacts on the surroundings) rather than "compatible" lists of uses aggregated in districts. Thus a restaurant or bar with live entertainment will have a much different impact on its neighbors than one with only a TV set.

C. **Increase hillside lot sizes.** As development creeps onto the hillsides, minimum lot sizes should be increased on a sliding scale proportional to the steepness of slope. Building coverage of the lot and height should also be carefully controlled to minimize disruption of the natural features of the site and adverse visual impacts, such as cutting off of views, light, air, and hilltops.

D. **Control signs.** A distinction should be made between signs that identify the business on a site and signs that simply use the community as a site for advertising products sold everywhere. Thus the tavern name on a sign should be given more consideration than the brand name sign for one of the beverages it sells. This also applies to national operations that use the entire building as a form of advertising. Many communities have successfully redirected the efforts of these corporations to impose their gross trademarks on the town center or its approaches. There is no constitutional right reserved for a plastic motel chain, quick hamburger franchise, or filling station empire to implant yet another of their standardized prefabricated carnival booths in your town.

Perhaps the classic example of firmness against corporate arrogance was the stand of 400-year-old Santa Fe, New Mexico, against the attempts of a national five-and-ten-cent store to erect its red sign with brass letters on a city plaza that had heard the hoofbeats of history clear back to the Spanish conquistadores. The ancient city was unbending against heavy pressure, and finally it got the corporation to put up a sign that harmonized with adobe and history. The rule made then has governed the city's attitude to other brash hucksters ever since. It is: "Our identity is more important than yours."

E. **Delegate downward.** Too many commissions are mired down by variances and use permits. If the state statutes do not require a zoning board of appeals (or adjustment), an ordinance creating a zoning administrator is advisable. The zoning administrator will do the job of holding hearings and making findings on hardship or justification for special permits. There are several advantages to this arrangement. It will lighten the planning commission's agenda. The public benefits in that its applications are not lost in the welter of commission business but are handled by a paid employee who can schedule hearings as frequently as the law allows. Moreover, the zoning administrator should be an expert on the zoning ordinance and able to interpret it on the spot for the public, the zoning enforcement officer, or the building inspector. A good zoning administrator can head off unnecessary applications for variances and misunderstandings of the regulations.

A zoning administrator is usually freer from political pressures than a planning commission or board of zoning appeals. As an employee of the planning department, the zoning administrator is far less likely to take an independent direction on variances and permits than an autonomous board of appeals or adjustment.

F. **Establish design or architectural review boards.** One of the very important jobs of development control is the protection and improvement of community appearance and amenity. Architectural review is often an activity that consumes too much commission time compared to what is achieved. While an amateur commission can deny approval to poor designs, it can rarely show an applicant what direction to take for improving a project so that it can be approved. A good design review board can do this. It should be made up of local architects and builders who can understand the standards new

123

developments must meet. They should also be able to suggest various approaches or guidelines for an applicant to use in improving a project. Commissions that suffer from accusations of being "antibusiness" when they try to prevent architectural mistakes ought to delegate this function to a group of professionals. This is particularly important in communities where the professional staff has no design training or where there is no professional staff.

Some of the things architectural or design review boards should focus on are:

1. Relationship to surroundings: Is the new structure a good neighbor to earlier structures? Is it in scale, harmonious in bulk, height, landscaping, and colors?

2. Protection of amenities: Are views, vistas, public spaces, pedestrian pathways, and important signs left clear? Are historic landmarks and areas disrupted? Does the structural treatment or site development create an unsafe area (too many driveways, blank walls, dark areas at night) or an unpleasant zone with noise, fumes, glare, smells, litter, or garbage? (This is a particular problem with take-out food shops.)

3. Review and advise before a design is complete is much the best policy. Consultation in the initial stages depends on the creation of a clear overview of what the review process is trying to achieve, and a detailed set of criteria for the design controls in each area of the community.

4. Design review is best used in limited areas of major importance, such as central business districts, historical preservation zones, and viewsheds, where strong design controls can be clearly tied to a public purpose.

5. The design review section of the zoning ordinance should provide for appeals from the review board to the legislative body rather than the planning commission, because the commission, like the review board, is simply another citizens' advisory board. An appeal is usually based on fairness, reasonableness, or practicality. These are problems whose solution is basically political and therefore they belong on the agenda of the elected politicians.

6. Design review should not go beyond questions of architectural merit. For example, the design review process should not get into questions of whether a use is in a proper

location. This is a zoning question and it belongs on the agenda of the planning commission.

7. The design review board should publish and distribute a design guide with its standards, policies, and criteria for site and building evaluation.

Subdivisions and Lot Splits

The principal responsibilities of the planning commission in subdivision regulation are:

A. Protection of the public interest in seeing that:

1. New developments pay for the costs they create.

2. The project does not disrupt existing services (e.g., overburden existing roads, utilities, schools) or diminish the environmental quality of the area (excessive cuts and fills, removal of trees, despoilation of streams, lakes, habitats).

3. The subdivision doesn't create health or safety hazards by building in landslide areas, flood plains, or soils with poor percolation, when septic tanks are proposed.

B. Provision for the future:

1. The subdivision should provide the required rights-of-way for the major street network[17] of the community. It should also set aside sites for needed public facilities such as schools, parks, and firehouses, which will be needed to serve the occupants of the development when it's completed. The general location of these sites should have been foreseen by the community's comprehensive plan.

2. Urbanization should not be allowed to take place at rural standards. Unpaved roads, failing wells, septic tanks, and open drainage ditches may work for a while for the first developer to break into an outlying area, but unless the density is low enough to ensure the perpetuation of the rural character of an area, further development usually shifts the costs of remedying the deficiencies onto the residents later

---

[17] The major street network is nowadays a portion of the transportation element of the comprehensive plan. It should map out in advance the hierarchy of streets and highways to correct existing congestion and extend the system into areas of future growth.

on. These are costs that are most often much higher than they would have been initially.

C. Need and timing:

Is the type of housing the development will provide in over-supply? Will it maintain a balance of housing opportunities for all segments of the community—poor as well as rich, families as well as the childless and single, the elderly as well as the youthful and middle-aged? Premature speculative subdivisions create isolated streets, scattered housing, and failing homeowners' association facilities such as recreation centers, golf courses, and parks. All of this adds to the tax burden of the community without offsetting revenues.

Recreational subdivisions: Second home subdivisions that sell lots for investment rather than primary home sites have been a particularly obnoxious problem in many areas. *Promised Lands, Subdivision in Deserts and Mountains* and *Subdividing Rural America* (by the ASPO Research staff) both found that the most serious negative impacts of recreational subdivisions came from the inadequacy or total lack of water, roads, and sewers. Moreover some locations were in environments completely unsuitable for intensive development. Take the typical (but fictional) Rancho Caliente, for example:

In 1½ years the developers filed 3,937 lots requiring 62 miles of private roads and 23 miles of public roads to be accepted by the county when they were built. A pool, tennis courts, club house, and horse stable were built to lure prospective buyers who were promised an active, thriving community in addition to lake fishing and the peace and serenity of the remote countryside. Eight years after the first unit had been offered for sale, only 92 homes had been built. At this rate the subdivision would take 345 years to build out. The pool and tennis courts were in need of repairs; the stables had closed. There was no health care or shopping in the immediate vicinity. Finally a class action suit brought by property owners against the developers' fraudulent sales practices got $30,000,000 returned to the lot buyers.

One has to ask where was the county planning process during this consumer fraud and environmental destruction? Anyone with a semblance of local knowledge could have foreseen that consumer protection, land and timber conservation, and the local tax rate required turning such a blue sky land promotion

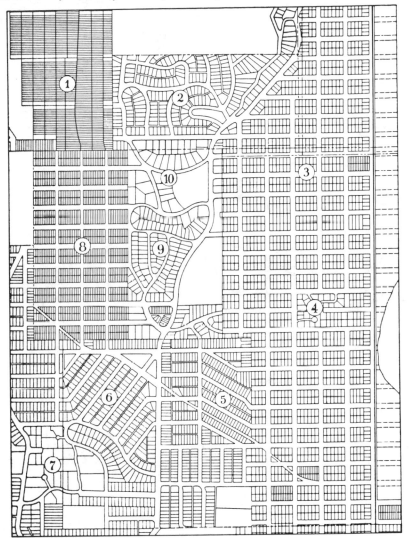

Many different types of subdivisions are represented in the above exhibit

1 A subdivision without streets: 25 foot lots.

2 Curvilinear streets—an attempt to fit the terrain.

3 Simple rectangular scheme—excess area in streets —bad grades.

4 Resubdivisions to secure better street grades and salable lots.

5 An angular pattern based upon an old narrow road.

6 Further attempts to meet topographic conditions—note long blocks.

7 Large lots—streets minimized.

8 Small lots, streets wide in one direction, narrow in another.

9 Large lots, long blocks, varied street widths; an attempt to develop all assets of property.

10 Lots and developments suited to area, but hemmed in by inappropriate schemes of development.

FIGURE 3

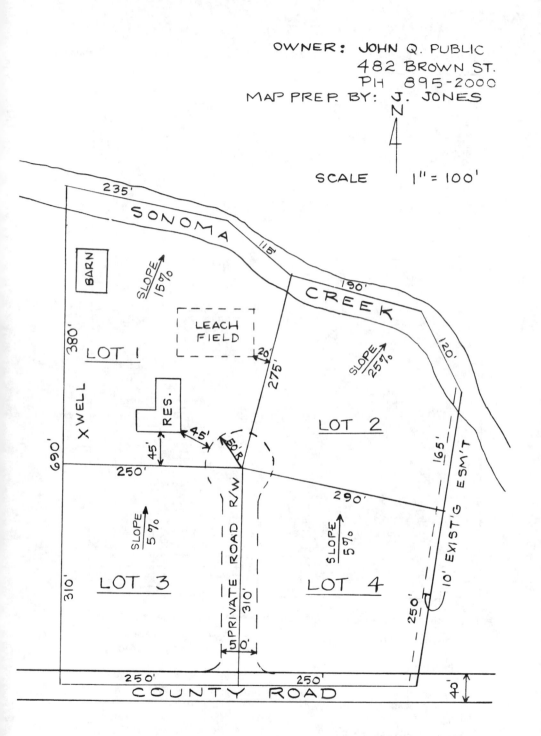

FIGURE 4. Sample lot-split map.

down. Local governments that can't use the police powers delegated to them any better than this example can expect the state and federal government to replace them.

D. Location:

Does this subdivision fit into the existing pattern of streets and utilities of the surrounding area? (See Figure 3.) Is it part of a compact extension of the community or does it leapfrog out into the countryside, requiring expensive extensions of roads, utilities, and urban services whose cost may be shifted onto the general tax base?

Lot splits: In many jurisdictions, lot jobbers evade the requirements of the subdivision regulations by selling off lots on a piecemeal basis, each land division creating one less lot than the number legally defined as a subdivision. Cumulatively, lot splits can quickly transform a fringe area from open countryside to a semiurbanized running sore unless this loophole is quickly closed.

Lot-split ordinances should be employed for any subdivision of property into two or more parcels. (See Figure 4.) Normally a lot-split ordinance should aim at making lot-split subdividers pay for their share of public improvements rather than deferring these costs for the homeowner to pay later. It's only fair for lot splitters to provide needed improvements for their customers just as the people who create conventional subdivisions do. Another reason for adopting a lot-split ordinance is to avoid having the residents and businesses who paid for their share of the cost of public improvements in a community unfairly taxed to build streets and drains in other parts of the community where they weren't provided initially. A second advantage of regulating lot splits is to avoid the "landlocked" condition of interior lands in rural areas when splitting along existing road frontages occurs without regard to access to adjacent properties. A ribbon of lot splits along an existing road also creates unsafe turning movements into individual driveways all along the road, rather than street intersections that can be controlled for safety and more efficient traffic movement.

Planned Unit Developments

Conventional subdivisions have usually been strips of lots set along ribbons of streets. Even when intervening property separated one from the other, it was almost always vacant real estate awaiting its turn with the bulldozer rather than permanent open space. Then in the sixties the housing industry turned to a new kind of land planning: the planned unit development (PUD). Its predominant features are:

☐ Smaller private yards as a result of clustering home sites with smaller networks of utilities and streets.

☐ Large common open areas and recreation centers, usually maintained by a private homeowners' association. (A homeowners' association is an incorporated nonprofit organization operating under recorded land agreements; each lot owner in the development is automatically a member of the association and is charged for his proportionate share of the association's costs in maintaining the communal facilities and open spaces.)

☐ The developments usually consist of owner-occupied single-family homes, townhouses, and a variety of other uses such as offices, shopping centers, and schools, which tend to make the larger developments self-sufficient.

There are also special problems for jurisdictions not thoroughly experienced in regulating them. They include:

☐ Many zoning and subdivision ordinances simply do not have any relevant standards for clustering or the mix of uses on a single tract of land that characterizes a PUD. (See Figure 5.)

☐ Planned unit developments are riskier than conventional subdivisions in that the recreation centers, golf courses, and open-space maintenance costs may be too much for the developer to bear if home sales are too slow, or may be more than the homeowners' association can or desires to pay for once it's all theirs. Then the pressure is put on the local government either to support these facilities with public funds or to allow development of the open lands and commercialization of the community recreation center.

☐ To test the market, the developer will usually start with but a single phase of a larger planned unit. In marketing the home sites, he may find that conditions have not met expectations or have changed, and the original approved plan must be amended. For the local planning commission this may mean starting all over again, especially if the commission membership has changed since the initial approval.

☐ The number of dwelling units a developer should be allowed to place on his land is very difficult to determine when there is a wide variation in the size of units and the number of occupants in each type. For small jurisdictions without sophisticated staff support, there is a danger that a commission will move away from quantitative controls and approve the development on the basis of its design features, the success of the developer's sales pitch, or on some other subjective basis that will allow overbuilding on the site.

☐ A favorite trick of less scrupulous developers is to offer the unbuildable "waste" land on the plot as "open space" (steep slopes, flood plains, gulleys, and even former gravel pits) in order to increase the density of development on the more easily managed parts of the property.

Regulating PUDs: The planned unit development process involves much more negotiation between the community and the developer than conventional tract developments. In order to make the negotiations balanced, the community needs:

a. Carefully drafted procedural guidelines including a combined zoning and subdivision ordinance for PUD development applications to reduce processing time.

b. Professional persons either as staff or design review board members to review the development design.

 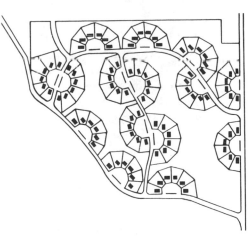

FIGURE 5. Conventional subdivision versus cluster subdivision design.

c. A good grasp on how a PUD will relate to the community's general plan. Is the plan flexible enough to work with market shifts in housing demand? Are planned public facility and utility systems adequate for PUD densities?

d. To know how effective the homeowner association will be in the future when the facilities they manage will need repairs, more maintenance, and more funds. Might the public be asked to take over the development? If there is such a possibility, then would the development make a good public facility in terms of the interests of the community?

Commissions reviewing a planned unit development should check the following special points:

1. Site plans, floor plans, and elevations for all structures to be established on the site; all landscaping existing on the land as well as that to be installed; trails, paths, bikeways, and all other access relating the homes to the open spaces and common recreational areas. This should be done at a public hearing on the "master plan" for the PUD which will settle what the completed development will look like even though the developer may only be proposing to build a single phase of it at this time. The initial stage should be sufficient unto itself in terms of access, circulation, drainage, open space, and other public facilities, so that the community will not wind up with a deficient housing tract if the subsequent phases don't materialize.

2. The community's zoning and subdivision ordinances should set forth the criteria for PUDs. PUDs should have direct access to major streets rather than allowing traffic from the PUD to filter through minor residential streets or undeveloped rural roads. (In some cases, the developer may have to contribute to offsite access improvements to make his project feasible.) In addition, the comprehensive plan should indicate the open spaces desired by the community so that the pieces dedicated by a PUD will fit into the pattern of trails, greenbelts, and environmental preserves desired by the community as a whole. Schools, parks, and other public facilities to serve the PUD and its surrounding area should be located in sufficient detail to enable them to be preserved from preemption by development until they are needed.

3. PUDs should be located in relation to public services and utility extensions so that no additional public costs are shifted onto the general taxpayer as a result of the community's taking

132

on the obligation of serving the development. An objective cost-benefit or economic impact analysis may be prudent insurance to protect the taxpayers of the jurisdiction from finding the spillover costs of a PUD added to their tax bills.

4. PUDs should be treated as an amendment of the zoning map conditioned by the deed restrictions, agreements for maintenance by the homeowners' association of common facilities and open spaces, and guarantees (surety bonds, etc.) by the developer for the completion of the development in accordance with the approved master plan and such detailed plans as are required, and finally, an agreement binding successors who may take over the completion of the development to the conditions of the plan approval. (This last is a very important point to insist upon.) Although lawyers often argue otherwise, it is unwise for a community to depart from the principle that land-use regulation runs with the land, not the ownership. When considering an amendment of the zoning map, only a preliminary plan of the PUD should be required. It should show the number of residential units, the circulation layout, and other uses on the property. The approval of this plan should be based on findings of zoning suitability, as with any other change of zone. At the hearing and in the notice of hearing, it should be made absolutely clear to the public that the hearing is going to be limited to zoning considerations and that only if the PUD's zoning is approved will final plans be required and reviewed.

If at all possible, the commission should consider discussion of design details of buildings, landscaping, and site layout[18] as irrelevant at the zoning change hearing. It might help, though, to let the public express its environmental and design concerns after all testimony on the proposed change to the planned development district has been received. Conversely, the commission should be alert to attempts to sell bad zoning on the basis of the attractiveness of the project (e.g., artists' renderings of lovely villas in impossibly rustic settings), hopeful projections of favorable tax benefits, and similar sales materials.

5. Part of the commission's findings in conditioning the approval of a PUD zone for a development should be recommended

[18] By the same token, the developer should not have to undergo the considerable expense of preparing detailed plans until the zoning has been approved by the council or board of supervisors.

modifications in the preliminary plan. In essence, there should be guidelines for the final plan submission, so that the developer doesn't have to keep going back to the drawing board before being allowed to build.

Condominiums: A relatively new form of homeownership, condominium housing has several potential problem areas with which commissions need to concern themselves. Chief among these is whether proper provision has been made by the developer for an adequate management program (including its funding) until enough units have been sold so that a homeowners' association may feasibly take over. Where sales have been slow, some developers have bailed out of even minimum upkeep after the initial period of intensive selling.

Another problem is the condominium conversion whereby existing rental apartments are converted from rental units under single ownership to individually owned condominium units. Condo-conversion (the term used in real estate jargon for the process of changing ownership status) is expected to continue to expand because:

a. The aggregate price for condominiums usually exceeds the sum for which the apartment building can be sold as an entity.

b. Apartment owners caught in the cost squeeze of higher operation and maintenance expenses, taxes, increased competition from newer units, and sometimes local rent controls find that condo-conversion offers an attractive way of bailing out of a tight financial situation.

c. Shortages of land zoned for multi-family use, loan money at reasonable interest rates, and skyrocketing construction and land costs have diverted developers' efforts to the more easily accomplishable conversion of existing buildings to condominiums.

Local concerns in regulation of this process are:

Both tenants and prospective purchasers need protection. For tenants being displaced by the conversion, substitute housing at rents they can afford to pay may be scarce, particularly for the elderly and low-income families with children. The desirability of a conversion proposal should be weighed in part by whether or not an adequate supply of relocation housing is available for the renters that would be displaced.

In many states buyer protection laws may already prevent abuses, but the local commission should at least require that approval of a conversion (usually handled as a subdivision) include: Required work to bring the building up to local codes be done prior to units being offered for sale. The seller should prepare a "full disclosure" report on the property (e.g., property taxes to be paid by condominium owners, deficiencies in the project, availability of shopping, schools, medical facilities) and most importantly, the terms and charges for the homeowners' association taking over the management and maintenance of the building. The commission should be satisfied that the arrangements for stewardship of the project during the interim period between single owner and full condominium status are adequate. A bond for a period of a year or two guaranteeing management and maintenance by the seller is advisable.

A tenant protection ordinance may be worthwhile where the rental housing inventory is low. It should include provisions for notification of tenants of a proposed condominium conversion before a tentative subdivision map is considered; it should require the developer to give the tenants a first refusal offer for purchase of the units. Evictions should not take place until at least ninety days after notification of the approval of the conversion proposal, and this approval should require that the developer pay a reasonable amount of moving expenses ($150-$200) for moves initiated after this notification. Denial of conversions when relocation housing is unavailable will probably be legally supportable on the grounds that creating hardships for displaced tenants is contrary to the public interest. This means that the city has a responsibility to monitor the availability of rental housing by rent level and tenant suitability.

Some cities have developed programs that protect tenants and preserve affordable rental housing. Many have restricted conversions by imposing automatic moratoriums when the rental vacancy level drops to a certain percentage of the rental housing stock.

San Francisco passed a law in 1979 that went far beyond what most cities have done. This law's major features were:

a. At least 40 percent of the tenants in every proposed conversion must sign an intent to purchase agreement before the proposal will be approved.

b. There must be life leases for the elderly.

c. Where the units are rented to moderate- or low-income tenants, the sales price cannot be set any higher than two and one-half times the upper income limit of the low- to moderate-income families occupying the property.

d. Converters of all condos must reserve at least 10 percent of the units for low- or moderate-income tenants. If more than 10 percent of the units are low- or moderate-income rentals, then the conversion must reserve the higher percentage. Developers can meet this requirement by constructing the required number of low- or moderate-income units in areas which do not already have assisted housing or by contributing an amount of money (determined by a city formula) to the city's Housing Development Fund, which is earmarked for the provision of low- and moderate-income housing.

e. Conversions of all types are limited to no more than 1,000 units per year.[19]

Regulating complex development projects: Once development becomes too complex to be regulated by an ordinance listing compatible uses and building standards, the planning agency and commission have embarked into uncharted waters of regulation by negotiation rather than by rule book. This negotiation should begin well before a formal application is submitted.

First, the planning staff and the developer's team should preview what the project proposal is all about. Three things should be nailed down by these preapplication conferences.

a. **The information and fees that the developer will have to submit with an application:** The planners should be reasonable about how much detail and expense are really necessary for an initial review. One attorney was told his client would have to submit a surveyed map showing the exact location of every tree on the property with a trunk larger than 24 inches. "That imbecile turned us into midnite loggers!" he

[19] See Daniel Lauber, "Condominion Conversions," *Journal of Housing,* April 1980, for a description of measures local governments have taken to relieve the pain of condominium conversions.

relates. This information should be given in writing so that there are no delays in processing due to misunderstandings. The staff should be as specific as it can at the outset. The directions should eschew words like "adequate," "proper," and "suitable," and say, for example, that the grading plans shall be at a scale of 1″ = 200′ with a 5-foot contour interval depicted for both existing and future gradients with cross sections through the property's width and length every 100 feet, etc.

b. **The timing of the review process:** This should be realistically estimated, taking into consideration workloads of staff, lead times necessary for noticing and hearings, time for commission deliberation and reviewing modifications, and so on. A good staff person never puts the commission on the spot by promising to have them dash through a bitterly opposed 900-acre planned community project in one evening. Yet many planners may be offended at the commission that has received their boiled down staff report yet wishes to think for themselves, rather than hastily rubber stamping staff's recommendations.

c. **The developer should be given a clear idea of what current policies, thinking, and reservations apply to the project as presented.** As many technical, land-use, and design problems as possible should be ironed out long before the project sees the light of a hearing room. Many engineers, attorneys, and others representing developers expect a paint-by-the-numbers project fix-up kit from their colleagues in public service. Many things that will put a project in the midst of conflict are not spelled out in ordinances or enumerated in codes. For example, some communities may have a civic self-image of a suburban village and anything that smacks too much of "big-city scale" will be in trouble from the outset, as any developer who was the first to propose a high-rise among ranch-style single-family tracts has learned. The high-rise may have a lower overall density, save open space, utilize energy more efficiently, provide affordable housing for residents, and do any number of good things, but if people decide that "I don't want to look at that damn thing every time I come home," it will probably not fly unless a city council majority wishes to make this term their last.

The following steps should be taken when you are holding a set of plans in your hands on the site (see Plates 1–4):

a. Visit the site with the plans and find out where things will be on the ground.

b. Check the scale of the plans. How large is a building compared with the size of a person or an auto? Draw one of each on the site and building plans.

c. Study the proposed contours compared with the existing ones. Is there a lot of grading proposed? Will the new contours follow the natural lay of the land or will there be straight cuts?

d. Locate existing trees, streams, and other natural features. How many trees will be saved? How much of the natural character of the land will be saved, paved over, piped under? Are existing views preserved?

e. How do the proposed buildings relate to neighboring structures? Will the supermarket's trash compactor be next to the sleeping quarters of the nursing home? Will shadows be cast over people's yards? Is there going to be window-to-window visual contact?

f. How will the auto and pedestrian circulation system work? Are there points of conflict from turning movements into and out of the site? With bicycles and pedestrian paths? Are delivery vehicles mixed into passenger car areas, causing occasional blocking of lanes? Will it be safe to walk through to the proposed parking area at night? Are there walkways in the parking areas or do people have to walk between cars, cut across shrubbery, and dart out into hazardous moving traffic?

Project checklist: Here is a checklist a commissioner can use to evaluate whether a project proposal can be approved, needs conditions imposed, needs modification, or should be denied. Where a competent professional staff is available, responses to the items on this list should be part of a staff report. In cases where staff is not available, the commission might look to Environmental Impact Reports, data furnished by the applicant, or reports of impartial experts hired with fees imposed on the project. The ideal project from a public standpoint would meet the following criteria:

I. Plans and policies

a. The project fits in with established zoning patterns, neighborhood character, and general plan proposals for population growth, population distribution, and capital improvement staging.

b. It doesn't close off options for the acquisition of future public facility sites, roads, open space, etc. Such sites and rights-of-way should be reserved for a specific time period

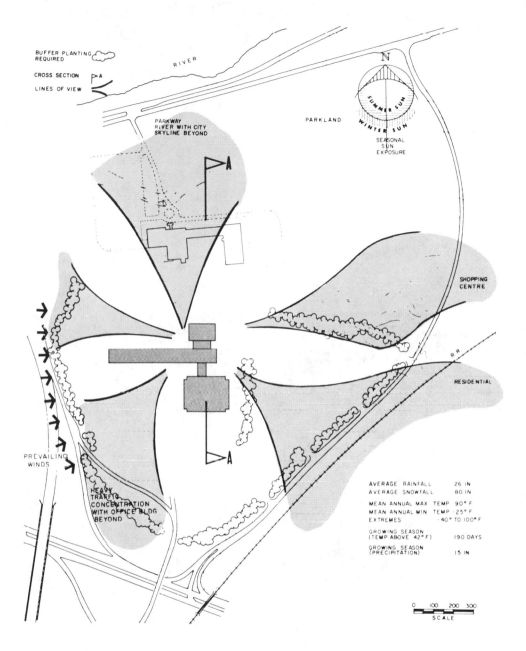

BUFFER PLANTING
REQUIRED

CROSS SECTION

LINES OF VIEW

RIVER

PARKWAY
RIVER WITH CITY
SKYLINE BEYOND

PARKLAND

N

SUMMER SUN

WINTER SUN

SEASONAL
SUN
EXPOSURE

A

SHOPPING
CENTRE

R R

RESIDENTIAL

PREVAILING
WINDS

HEAVY
TRAFFIC
CONCENTRATION
WITH OFFICE BLDG
BEYOND

A

AVERAGE RAINFALL   26 IN
AVERAGE SNOWFALL   80 IN

MEAN ANNUAL MAX TEMP 90° F
MEAN ANNUAL MIN TEMP 25° F
EXTREMES   -40° TO 100° F

GROWING SEASON
(TEMP ABOVE 42° F)   190 DAYS

GROWING SEASON
(PRECIPITATION)   15 IN

0   100   200   300
SCALE

PLATE 1: This site analysis for a building complex shows climatic conditions and views to be preserved and others to be screened. This is important in understanding whether building placement and landscaping are proper. (From *Landscape and Site Development*, prepared by the Design Branch, Department of Public Works, Ottawa, Canada.)

139

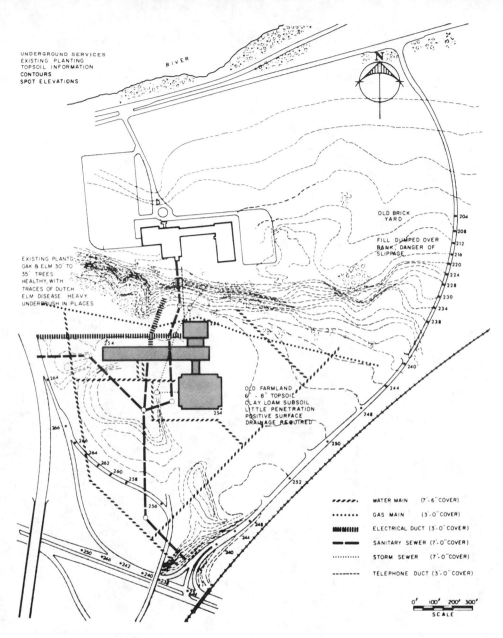

UNDERGROUND SERVICES
EXISTING PLANTING
TOPSOIL INFORMATION
CONTOURS
SPOT ELEVATIONS

RIVER

N

OLD BRICK
YARD

FILL DUMPED OVER
BANK, DANGER OF
SLIPPAGE

EXISTING PLANTG:
OAK B ELM 30' TO
35' TREES
HEALTHY, WITH
TRACES OF DUTCH
ELM DISEASE HEAVY
UNDERBRUSH IN PLACES

OLD FARMLAND
6" - 8" TOPSOIL
CLAY LOAM SUBSOIL
LITTLE PENETRATION
POSITIVE SURFACE
DRAINAGE REQUIRED

/////	WATER MAIN (7'-6" COVER)
••••••	GAS MAIN (3'-0" COVER)
▨▧▨	ELECTRICAL DUCT (3'-0" COVER)
▬ ▬ ▬	SANITARY SEWER (7'-0" COVER)
·········	STORM SEWER (7'-0" COVER)
--------	TELEPHONE DUCT (3'-0" COVER)

0' 100' 200' 300'
SCALE

PLATE 2: Site analysis for a building complex shows existing contours, landscaping, and the location of utilities — all very important for appreciating how development might change natural features, where easements will be required, and where landscaping is possible given existing soil conditions. (From *Landscape and Site Development,* prepared by the Design Branch, Department of Public Works, Ottawa, Canada.)

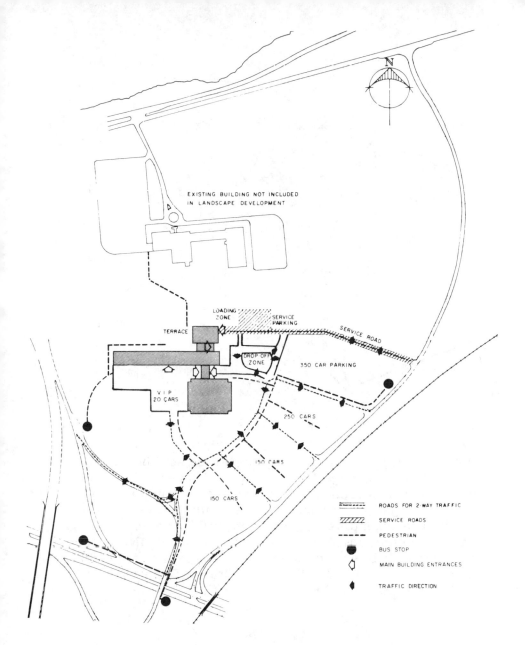

PLATE 3: This site analysis shows the proposed traffic pattern on the site. Where possible, existing traffic volumes, average daily traffic, and peak hour flows on the nearby streets should be shown so that the impact of the project's increment of additional traffic can be understood in terms of whether the local traffic system will be operating above or below peak capacities. The map is also useful in predicting potential problems, such as turning movements that might require signals. (From *Landscape and Site Development,* prepared by the Design Branch, Department of Public Works, Ottawa, Canada.)

141

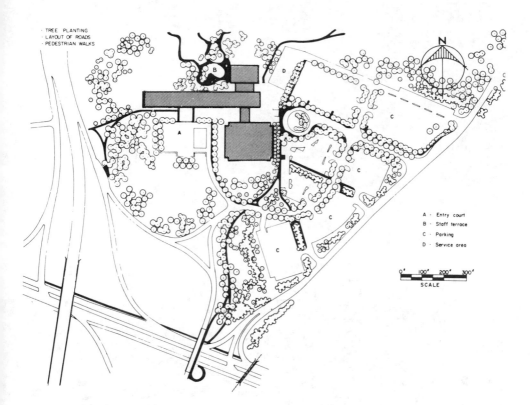

A · Entry court
B · Staff terrace
C · Parking
D · Service area

0' 100' 200' 300'
SCALE

PLATE 4: This proposed landscape design depicts the project on the site with buildings, landscaping, parking, and all the other improvements that will form the basis of the more detailed design. One problem of master plans like this one is that the landscaping may require twenty to thirty years to reach the proportions shown on this map. A three- to five-year tree size should be shown instead. (From *Landscape and Site Development,* prepared by the Design Branch, Department of Public Works, Ottawa, Canada.)

142

(e.g., two years) to allow public purchase; this should be made a condition of approval.

c. The project doesn't represent a major change in existing levels of service, jurisdictional operations, or fiscal stability.

d. If the area is not yet covered by an adopted plan, the project will not put irreversible limitations on the area as it is or on future plans for it. (A major residential development in an agricultural district may raise taxes on farms, impede their operation, and ultimately ruin the area for agriculture.)

II. Local effects

a. The project will not have a domino effect, in that it becomes the opening wedge for further rapid growth, urbanization, or other land-use change beyond what is indicated in a growth management or neighborhood plan.

b. It will not affect market values and/or tax rates of other nearby properties.

c. There is sufficient existing capacity in public services and facilities to accommodate this project. If new facilities will be required, the project will fully pay for them. It should also not require premature or expensive extra buyer's costs to operate facilities which would burden resident taxpayers in the future. For example, some "planned community" projects used recreation clubs with golf links, pools, saunas, indoor tennis courts, etc., as sales lures. Once the project was partially sold, the club facilities were left to the home buyers to support. Many times, a majority feel they cannot handle the spiraling costs on top of their mortgage and taxes, and an irresistible bloc of citizens gets the city or county to take their club into the public domain.

d. The project will generate its fair share of public facilities, open space, and recreation and school sites so that no burdens are placed on what the community already has in place.

e. It will be a good neighbor physically and socially and improve the cohesion and identity of the area.

III. Economic considerations

a. The project is realistic in terms of how much of the local or regional market it needs to capture so it can reach full development.

b. There is a demonstrable public need for the project and

143

there is not a large inventory of approved projects in the same market area at this time.

c. The applicant is really in a position to build the project as approved and is not just brokering the permits and project approval to others. Project approvals should be limited to a reasonable time span, such as two years for a simple project and up to four or five years for a complex one.

d. The project will reach full development as proposed in a reasonably short span of time and not be back again and again for more concessions because of changes in "market conditions."

IV. Displacement impacts

a. The project will not remove low- and moderate-income housing that is in short supply.

b. It will not remove businesses or facilities that will have difficulty relocating or being replaced. This is a major concern where public funds such as urban renewal or development bond money are used to subsidize a project.

c. The project will not impinge on established agricultural or rural enterprises in a detrimental way.

d. The project will not remove or irreparably damage any historical buildings or sites, significant landmarks, vistas, views, or trails.

V. Environmental criteria

a. The site is free from hazards from landslides, earthquakes, differential settling, serious erosion, flooding, fire, and storms.

b. The project is well clear or protected from manmade hazards such as noise (airport approaches, etc.), chemical waste dumps, blasting, dust (from quarrying, etc.), pesticide spraying, smoke, solid waste contaminants, polluted water supplies, radiation, and noxious smells.

c. The project does not create any of the above hazards in the community.

More complete checklists are given in Appendices C and D for those who wish to follow an Environmental Impact Report format.

144 **And a bit of philosophy to bring meaning to the job:** Most students of case law in planning and zoning find the legal

maxim of ancient Rome, *salus populai, lex suprema* ("the welfare of the people is the supreme law"), governing decisions on how far the police power may be extended over private property rights. However, in a free enterprise nation like the United States, we also subscribe to the idea that Adam Smith proposed in his *Wealth of Nations* — namely, that in pursuing his or her own interest, a person is promoting the welfare of all. This puts people who regulate private development in a double bind. If, on the one hand, they assume the mantle of dispensers of the supreme law, many soon embroil themselves in a self-proclaimed holy war against the greed and dishonesty of profit makers.[20]

On the other hand, some regulators believe that private endeavors are benignly guided by "an invisible hand" and that the market (or "supply side" as the Reagan economists put it) regulates itself to produce maximum returns. What this outlook fails to recognize is that while an entrepreneur may maximize visible personal returns under this type of regulation, there are uncompensated spillover costs to others. This was recognized as early as 1795 when a New Jersey court ruled against the diversion of a stream by stating that "It cannot be legally diverted from its course without the consent of all who have an interest in it."[21]

The trick then is to try to work with the development and use of the property so that it serves the public interest. The best advice on how to operate effectively in the middle ground between what is profitable to a developer and what is beneficial to the public was described in John A. Rohr's statement on values regarding the connection between property rights and the public interest:

The connection between property rights and the public interest has some bearing upon the discretionary judgments made by contemporary bureaucrats in regulatory agencies. For one thing, it underscores the futility of railing against

[20] There is some evidence for feeling uneasy about how law-abiding big business has been. *Fortune*, the magazine of business, stated that of 1,043 of the biggest major corporations studied, 117 or 11 percent have been involved in "blatant illegalities" (in the United States) in the past decade. A "blatant illegality" is defined as a successful federal case against the corporation. This excludes crimes committed abroad. (Irwin Ross, "How Lawless Are Big Companies?" *Fortune*, vol. 102, no. 11, December 1980.)

[21] *Merrit* v. *Parker* 1. N.J.L. 526 to 530.

"corporate greed." Perhaps the problem is not so much that corporations are greedy but that at times the wrong corporations with the wrong kinds of greed have been rewarded by public policy. For bureaucracts in regulatory agencies it might be wise not to fret over how to transform business executives into "industrial statesmen" whose "social awareness" will make them "sensitive" and "responsive" to the needs of the public. Rather, the proper course might be to regard corporate greed as a great national resource and to point this mighty engine in directions that are socially useful. There was a time when we were told that invisible hands and free markets would do this for us. In some instances this may still be true today, but the nature of the contemporary industrial-regulatory-welfare-warfare state seems to suggest that the very visible and at times quite heavy hand of government must pick up where its invisible mate left off. If so, it becomes important for bureaucrats to assume an aggressive stance toward the industries they regulate. They should look upon the interests of these industries, not as ends in themselves, but as instruments related to higher ends of public interest. By no means does this mean that the regulatory agencies need always and necessarily be hostile to the industries they regulate. It does mean they should be selective in the sort of activity that is encouraged, and such selective encouragement may well mean that some companies will prosper handsomely while promoting the public interest.

The ethical significance of all this is that it is not enough for the conscientious bureaucrat to adhere scrupulously to conflict-of-interest regulations. Although such fidelity is absolutely essential, it does no more than assure us that the bureaucrat is not the pawn of the companies he or she regulates. While this is a consummation devoutly to be wished, it ignores the more important question of how government can manipulate corporate property interests in a beneficial manner. This is the proper sphere of bureaucratic discretion in regulatory agencies. Not only must the regulatory agencies avoid being captured by the industries they regulate but they must also encourage, cajole, discipline, and exploit the acquisitive passions of the leaders of these industries in a way that will promote higher national goals.[22]

146   [22] John A. Rohr, *Ethics for Bureaucrats: An Essay on Law and Values* (New York: Marcell Dekker Inc., 1978). Used by permission.

Doing a Good Job on Small-Town and Rural Commissions

9

Let there be spaces in your togetherness.

—Kahlil Gibran

For most of the twentieth century the census has given us a picture of rural and small-town Americans moving to the big metropolitan areas. We all learned in school that it took fewer and fewer farm workers to feed the nation and a hungry world with each passing decade. Once in a while, someone would try to do something about the "dying small towns," such as the well-intentioned federal officials who gave Wink, Texas, a couple million dollars for revitalization in the early sixties. The result of the urban renewal corporation's purchase of homes and stores in this played-out oil town was that at last many of the inhabitants had enough cash to move on to greener pastures, and they did in droves. Today they might think differently about a move to the big city. For example, in 1978 the Louis Harris organization polled Americans on their views and concerns about urban life on behalf of the U.S. Department of Housing and Urban Development. The results were startling. Of those interviewed, 47 percent stated a preference for living in a rural area or small town not located in the suburbs, while only 16 percent stated a preference for living in a city with more than 250,000 people. *Time,* two years later, reported that instead of piling up in the suburbs, restless Americans were headed for the nonmetropolitan areas in record numbers with mixed results.

This demographic turnabout may have many meanings but one is already clear: The small town in America is once again on the rise. . . .

The small town as an ideal is familiar. The very notion as though invented by Norman Rockwell has always carried with it images of low-key living, easy friendships, neighborly neighbors, front-porch sociability, back-fence congeniality, downtown camaraderie. Small town – the phrase – evokes an intimate sense of community, leafy serenity free of the sinister strangers that menace the cold grimy canyons of the city. . . .

The typical small town is free of the city's unruly ambience, but not of its nagging problems. Small towns just like the cities struggle constantly with tight budgets and pressing needs that keep rising faster than revenues. . . .

While many small town are frantically trying to get more industry or keep what they have, others are groaning under the problem of providing services for the additional people who come in with new industry. Colorado's Governor Richard D. Lamm complained that the energy boom was bringing some of his small towns more prosperity than they could afford. Wrote Lamm, "Craig, Rifle, Meeker – towns that have existed on a stable agricultural base for 100 years – are doubling every two years, every three years. With that growth comes every social pathology; when Rifle doubles in size, juvenile delinquency increases three times; the alcoholism rate increases four times, displaced homemakers increase 4.5 times. The immediate costs are immense, the long term benefit doubtful." It is no wonder that some little communities . . . "struggle to stay small."[1]

Planning commissions in small towns and rural areas face special challenges which are unique to such places. A reasonably thorough coverage of small-town and rural planning would require a book twice the size of this one. Therefore it's the purpose of this chapter to highlight the major topics that people working with the planning of such areas should know about.

What the job's like: The commissioner new to small-town or rural planning should be willing to work under most of the following conditions:

[1] Frank Tippet, "Small Town, USA: Growing and Groaning," *Time,* September 1, 1980.

a. Sit through many meetings that are informal, repetitious, and very heated. It's important to give everyone a chance to have their say, even at the cost of efficient handling of applications.

b. Accept and work within a climate of public distrust of regulation, planning, and government in general. In many communities you should be able to do missionary work for planning in a climate of nineteenth-century cowboy land ethics and robber baron economic principles.

c. Be available and answerable at all times to politicians and local residents on every local issue, problem, and rumor. While it's generally considered illegal to have ex parte or outsider contacts on applications before the commission, people living in small communities cannot lock themselves away in seclusion like the jury in a murder trial. The important thing is to make sure that everyone who approaches you for an opinion or a sympathetic ear knows that you don't make up your mind until all the facts you're supposed to look at have been presented.

d. Help provide a planning function for your community with limited or dwindling funds, with a limited (or no) staff and an inadequate budget.

Staff: The most important thing about selecting a planner for small towns and rural areas (assuming an acceptable level of competency) is to be sure the planner can come to know and effectively work with the people he or she serves. The planner should be able to listen to people rather than always telling them what to do. In many cases a planner's personal style as "Expert Eddie" or "Gloria Grad-Student" will turn people in the community off. Universities need to be encouraged to offer programs that teach students how to communicate with the fifty-nine-year-old retired dairy farmer who is chairman of the Dinner Fork County Planning Commission.

If the planner becomes acceptable personally, he or she must then help to make planning acceptable. There are several ways to do this. For example, he could be of service to several special districts such as schools, water, research and development, and soil conservation by doing population and land analyses. In one county each of the above organizations was delighted to learn how many buildable vacant lots there were in their respective districts. This information was easily obtained from the county assessor's files with a few

149

programming innovations. The planner should find a way to become an accepted member of the community. One planner not only became an outstanding Little League coach, but also fed star players into his teams from his huge brood of children. When a cabal of new council members bandied his dismissal about, 500 names on a petition arrived denouncing the very thought! Most were from parents whose boys had benefited from his coaching skills.

A very good way to promote planning is to solve a problem that people can see right now. The planner might work with the chief of police to get a "massage parlor" ordinance on the books, or with the administration to get a grant for the new firehouse. In one city the county had bequested a 20-acre weed patch to the municipality as its park. It was the only park for 70,000 people living in a former agricultural valley. There wasn't enough money to make it usable, but there was some money to hire a noted architect to do a unique site plan. Each element of the plan was designed as a project that could be funded and installed by a local volunteer group. Thus the Rotary put in the benches and barbecues, the Water District installed the sprinkler system, the PTA gave the toddlers' play equipment, and so on. Planning thereby became a very visible and accepted part of that city.

No staff: Many rural counties and towns have planning commissions but no full-time planners to serve the communities' needs. There are several ways around this problem that have been successful.

a. **Rent a planner:** A planner from a nearby jurisdiction or consulting firm (but far enough away to avoid conflicting loyalties or interests) can be brought in to work on a case-by-case basis. Most of the costs of the planner's work on development review applications could come from the fees charged applicants.

b. **Circuit riders:** Several communities can hire a planner to serve each of them on a part-time basis, so that planning services are available to each for only a fraction of the cost of a full-time professional.

c. **Outside organizations:** Regional councils, universities, state planning agencies, and large counties can often contract or even offer for free staff services for things such as plan and ordinance preparation.

d. **Grow your own:** Very often intelligent and capable people are available for work on a subprofessional basis. With some additional training (and encouragement), such people can become valuable planning staff, covering many of the gaps left by not having a professional. For example, one small Missouri town found that the commission's secretary had an extensive big-city background as a paralegal assistant. With some additional training and pay incentives, she became a homegrown, excellent zoning administrator.

Training: Because rural and small-town commissioners and staff so often work in remote locations, it's essential that they receive as much group training as the budget will allow. Perhaps the most useful way to do this is to have local seminars and workshops focusing on what commissioners, staff, and other public officials need to know about the problems and needs they're currently confronting. A side benefit of having joint training with other local jurisdictions is that people who share common boundaries and problems can meet and learn from each other. To some extent the conferences held by state planning and local government organizations also offer commissioners from various places the opportunity to learn from informal as well as structured interchanges.

Many university extension programs provide short courses in subjects that staff and commissioners need to know for their work.

Some special tasks: The first special task of a small-town commission is to bring the general plan up to date. HUD provided millions of dollars for its 701 general plan preparation program in the sixties and early seventies. In many states practically every jurisdiction went out and got one as a prerequisite for getting other federal funds. Many of these were slapped together by dubious consultants and have been gathering dust since they arrived in the mail. Others have become obsolete. They don't address new goals and problems that have arisen since the plan was prepared, or they don't incorporate information from the latest census, recent sewage or energy plans, or new state legislation. Much of the data gathering and survey work can be done by volunteers guided by a work program carefully prepared by a professional. This is a good way to get citizens involved in the new plan, for they will learn what the nature and needs of the community are by enumerating them firsthand. Some of the more difficult work can be done by interns from a nearby planning school. If the relationship with the consultant who prepared the original plan is still close, he or she may be invited in to assist again and supervise local volunteer efforts.

The second special task is to make sure that the ordinances the community has are being enforced. This means getting some law and order (fines, penalties, and notices of violations by someone answerable to the commission). One of the hardest illegal activities to police in rural areas is "pyramid four-by-fours"—illegal subdivisions created by carving up land into four pieces over and over and recording lots in fictitious names so that major subdivision regulations are avoided. These lots are then peddled to real people who learn only too late that they've bought land without roads, water, utilities, or even enough perculation for a working septic tank.

Many states have seen their rural areas carved up into giant subdivisions and sold to people all over the nation as second-home sites, real estate investments, retirement centers, and master planned cities of the twenty-first century. Much of this $4-billion business is blatantly fraudulent. The state of New Mexico has had a great deal of experience with land frauds. A full description of a classic scheme is presented in Appendix E.[2]

---

[2] Justice sometimes catches up with the perpetrators of such schemes, as evidenced by the following story from *The Wall Street Journal* (May 5, 1981):

Washington — The Federal Trade Commission ordered Horizon Corp. to refund $14.5 million to about 40,000 customers who bought land based on what the FTC says were "false and misleading claims."

What's more, the commission's final order requires Horizon to make certain that it or some other developer spends $45 million during the next 20 years improving the land. These improvements are to include water and sewer service, roads and electricity hookups. Also, the FTC says Horizon must notify its customers that the undeveloped land in Arizona, Texas, and New Mexico has barely any resale value and that Horizon doesn't have any immediate plans to develop individual lots.

The commission's complaint was substantially upheld in 1979 by an administrative law judge, who ruled that Horizon had perpetrated a "vicious consumer fraud" in its high-pressure sales "of virtually worthless desert land." The hearing officer said the land, for which buyers paid an average of $3,200 a lot, "has little value as investments and little use as home sites." The practices violated the Federal Trade Commission Act, the hearing officer ruled.

If a land-sale scheme proposed in your area smacks of fraud, do the following:

a. Check with HUD, the Office of Interstate Land Sales Registration, the Better Business Bureau, and the real estate commission to learn the reputation of the developer.

b. Require performance bonds guaranteeing completion of all improvements.

c. Check the written disclosure statement (required by law in many states) to be given to potential buyers for accuracy.

d. Get an ordinance prohibiting misrepresentation in the advertising of subdivided land.

e. Check with your local district attorney to learn whether deceptive practices and promotion of land as a "good investment" are covered by State Unfair Practices and Securities Acts.

Try to work with the special land-use and economic problems of farmers. A problem that is usually more prevalent than fraud is the conflict between agriculture and urbanization. Many jurisdictions feel that they can preserve agriculture by merely zoning the land for agriculture. This predicament is described by the old proverb, "Farmers live poor but die rich." Much of the net worth of farmers is tied up in their land, and their retirement plan is to make the last crop—real estate. Planning should be fair to farmers in the following ways:

a. They should be sheltered from having to pay for urban services from which they do not benefit. This is the main objective of agricultural preserve zoning and tax relief schemes that tax on use value rather than market value.

b. If the farmer does not have a family member who wishes to continue farming, then the farm should be sheltered from estate taxes when it is purchased by another person who will farm.

c. Decision makers in rural areas need to learn that the preservation of prime forests and farmlands is the only way for our society to keep its options open. This means that conservation and proper management of the natural resources of a rural area are very much a priority for rural planning.

The Land Conservation and Development Commission (LCDC) of Oregon set up some excellent guidelines for planning in this area of concern. They are reproduced here with the suggestion that they not be copied but rather studied as a model for structuring a local rural planning program with its own priorities.

Agricultural Lands

Goal: *To preserve and maintain agricultural lands.*

Agriculture lands shall be preserved and maintained for farm use, consistent with existing and future needs for agricultural products, forest, and open space. These lands shall be inventoried and preserved by adopting exclusive farm use zones pursuant to ORS Chapter 215. Such minimum lot sizes as are utilized for any farm use zones shall be appropriate for the continuation of the existing commercial agricultural enterprise with the area. Conversion of rural agricultural land to urbanizable land shall be based upon consideration of the following factors: (1) environmental, energy, social, and economic consequences; (2) demonstrated need consistent with LCDC goals; (3) unavailability of an alternative suitable location for the requested use; (4) compatibility of the proposed use with related agricultural land; and (5) the retention of Class I, II, III, and IV soils in farm use. A governing body proposing to convert rural agricultural land to urbanizable land shall follow the procedures and requirements set forth in the Land Use Planning goal (Goal 2) for goal exceptions.

Agricultural Land—*In western Oregon is land of predominantly Class I, II, III, and IV soils and in eastern Oregon is land of predominantly Class I, II, III, IV, V, and VI soils as identified in the Soil Capability Classification System of the United States Soil Conservation Service, and other lands which are suitable for farm use taking into consideration soil fertility, suitability for grazing, climatic conditions, existing and future availability of water for farm irrigation purposes, existing land-use patterns, technological and energy inputs required, or accepted farming practices. Lands in other classes which are necessary to permit farm practices to be undertaken on adjacent or nearby lands, shall be included as agricultural land in any event.*

More detailed soil data to define agricultural land may be utilized by local governments if such data permits achievement of this goal.

154

Farm Use — *is as set forth in ORS 215.203 and includes the nonfarm uses authorized by ORS 215.213.*

Guidelines:

A. Planning

1. Urban growth should be separated from agricultural lands by buffer or transitional areas of open space.

2. Plans providing for the preservation and maintenance of farmland for farm use should consider as a major determinant the carrying capacity of the air, land, and water resources of the planning area. The land conservation and development actions provided for by such plans should not exceed the carrying capacity of such resources.

B. Implementation:

1. Nonfarm uses permitted within farm use zones under ORS 215.213 (2) and (3) should be minimized to allow for maximum agricultural productivity.

2. Extension of services, such as sewer and water supplies, into rural areas should be appropriate for the needs of agriculture, farm use, and nonfarm uses established under ORS 215.213.

3. Services that need to pass through agricultural lands should not be connected with any use that is not allowed under ORS 215.203 and 215.213, should not be assessed as part of the farm unit, and should be limited in capacity to serve specific service areas and identified needs.

4. Forest and open space uses should be permitted on agricultural land that is being preserved for future agricultural growth. The interchange of such lands should not be subject to tax penalties.

Forest Lands

Goal: *To conserve forest lands for forest uses.*

Forest land shall be retained for the production of wood fiber and other forest uses. Lands suitable for forest uses shall be inventoried and designated as forest lands. Existing forest land uses shall be protected unless proposed changes are in conformance with the comprehensive plan.

In the process of designating forest lands, comprehensive plans shall include the determination and mapping of forest site classes according to the United States Forest Service manual "Field Instructions for Integrated Forest Survey and Timber Management Inventories — Oregon, Washington and California, 1974."

Forest Lands — are (1) lands composed of existing and potential forest lands which are suitable for commercial forest uses; (2) other forested lands needed for watershed protection, wildlife and fisheries habitat, and recreation; (3) lands where extreme conditions of climate, soil, and topography require the maintenance of vegetative cover irrespective of use; (4) other forested lands in urban and agricultural areas which provide urban buffers, wind breaks, wildlife, and fisheries habitat, livestock habitat, scenic corridors, and recreational use.

Forest Uses — are (1) the production of trees and the processing of forest products; (2) open space, buffers from noise, and visual separation of conflicting uses; (3) watershed protection and wildlife and fisheries habitat; (4) soil protection from wind and water; (5) maintenance of clean air and water; (6) outdoor recreational activities and related support services and wilderness values compatible with these uses; and (7) grazing land for livestock.

Guidelines:

A. Planning:

1. Forest lands should be inventoried so as to provide for the preservation of such lands for forest uses.

2. Plans providing for the preservation of forest lands for forest uses should consider as a major determinant the carrying capacity of the air, land, and water resources of the planning area. The land conservation and development actions provided for such plans should not exceed the carrying capacity of such resources.

B. Implementation:

1. Before forest land is changed to another use, the productive capacity of the land in each use should be considered and evaluated.

2. Developments that are allowable under the forest lands classification should be limited to those activities for forest

production and protection and other land management uses that are compatible with forest production. Forest lands should be available for recreation and other uses that do not hinder growth.

3. Forestation or reforestation should be encouraged on land suitable for such purposes, including marginal agricultural land not needed for farm use.

4. Road standards shold be limited to the minimum width necessary for management and safety.

5. Highways through forest lands should be designed to minimize impact on such lands.

6. Rights-of-way should be designed so as not to preclude forest growth whenever possible.

7. Maximum utilization of utility rights-of-way should be required before permitting new ones.

8. Comprehensive plans should consider other land uses that are adjacent to forest lands so that conflicts with forest harvest and management are avoided.

Open Spaces, Scenic and Historic Areas, and Natural Resources

Goal: To conserve open space and protect natural and scenic resources.

Programs shall be provided that will: (1) insure open space, (2) protect scenic and historic areas and natural resources for future generations, and (3) promote healthy and visually attractive environments in harmony with the natural landscape character. The location, quality, and quantity of the following resources shall be inventoried:

a. Land needed for desirable for open space;

b. Mineral and aggregate resources;

c. Energy sources;

d. Fish and wildlife areas and habitats;

e. Ecologically and scientifically significant natural areas, including desert areas;

f. Outstanding scenic views and sites;

157

g. Water areas, wetlands, watersheds, and groundwater resources;

h. Wilderness areas;

i. Historic areas, sites, structures, and objects;

j. Cultural areas;

k. Potential and approved Oregon recreation trails;

l. Potential and approved federal wild and scenic waterways and state scenic waterways.

Where no conflicting uses for such resources have been identified, such resources shall be managed so as to preserve their original character. Where conflicting uses have been identified, the economic, social, environmental, and energy consequences of the conflicting uses shall be determined and programs developed to achieve the goal.

Cultural Area —refers to an area characterized by evidence of an ethnic, religious, or social group with distinctive traits, belief and social forms.

Historic Areas —are lands with sites, structures, and objects that have local, regional, statewide, or national historical significance.

Natural Area —includes land and water that has substantially retained its natural character and land and water that, although altered in character, is important as habitats for plant, animal, or marine life, for the study of its natural historical, scientific, or paleontological features, or for the appreciation of its natural features.

Open Space —consists of lands used for agricultural or forest uses, and any land area that would, if preserved and continued in its present use:

a. Conserve and enhance natural or scenic resources;

b. Protect air or streams or water supply;

c. Promote conservation of soils, wetlands, beaches, or tidal marshes;

d. Conserve landscaped areas, such as public or private golf courses, that reduce air pollution and enhance the value of abutting or neighboring property;

e. Enhance the value to the public of abutting or neighboring *parks, forests, wildlife preserves, nature reservations or sanctuaries, or other open space;*

f . *Promote orderly urban development.*

Scenic Areas —*are lands that are valued for their aesthetic appearance.*

Wilderness Areas —*are areas where the earth and its community of life are untrammeled by man, where man himself is a visitor who does not remain. It is an area of undeveloped land retaining its primeval character and influence, without permanent improvement or human habitation, which is protected and managed so as to preserve its natural conditions and which (1) generally appears to have been affected primarily by the forces of nature, with the imprint of man's work substantially unnoticeable; (2) has outstanding opportunities for solitude or a primitive and unconfined type of recreation; (3) may also contain ecological, geological, or other features of scientific, educational, scenic, or historic value.*

Guidelines:

A. Planning:

1. *The need for open space in the planning area should be determined, and standards developed for the amount, distribution, and type of open space.*

2. *Criteria should be developed and utilized to determine what uses are consistent with open space values and to evaluate the effect of converting open space lands to inconsistent uses. The maintenance and development of open space in urban areas should be encouraged.*

3. *Natural resources and required sites for the generation of energy (i.e., natural gas, oil, coal, hydro, geothermal, uranium, solar, and others) should be conserved and protected; reservoir sites should be identified and protected against irreversible loss.*

4. *Plans providing for open space, scenic and historic areas, and natural resources should consider as a major determinant the carrying capacity of the air, land, and water resources of the planning area. The land conservation and development actions provided for by such plans should not exceed the carrying capacity of such resources.*

5. The National Register of Historic Places and the recommendations of the State Advisory Committee on Historic Preservation should be utilized in designating historic sites.

6. In conjunction with the inventory of mineral and aggregate resources, sites for removal and processing of such resources should be identified and protected.

7. As a general rule, plans should prohibit outdoor advertising signs except in commercial or industrial zones. Plans should not provide for the reclassification of land for the purpose of accommodating an outdoor advertising sign. The term "outdoor advertising sign" has the meaning set forth in ORS 377.710(23).

B. Implementation:

1. Development should be planned and directed so as to conserve the needed amount of open space.

2. The conservation of both renewable and nonrenewable natural resources and physical limitations of the land should be used as the basis for determining the quantity, quality, location, rate, and type of growth in the planning area.

3. The efficient consumption of energy should be considered when utilizing natural resources.

4. Fish and wildlife areas and habitats should be protected and managed in accordance with the Oregon Wildlife Commission's fish and wildlife management plans.

5. Stream flow and water levels should be protected and managed at a level adequate for fish, wildlife, pollution abatement, recreation, aesthetics, and agriculture.

6. Significant natural areas that are historically, ecologically, or scientifically unique, outstanding, or important, including those identified by the State Natural Area Preserves Advisory Committee, should be inventoried and evaluated. Plans should provide for the preservation of natural areas consistent with an inventory of scientific, educational, ecological, and recreational needs for significant natural areas.

7. Local, regional, and state governments should be encouraged to investigate and utilize fee acquisition,

*easements, cluster developments, preferential
assessment, development rights acquisition, and similar
techniques to implement this goal.*

8. *State and federal agencies should develop statewide
natural resource, open space, scenic and historic area
plans and provide technical assistance to local and
regional agencies. State and federal plans should be
reviewed and coordinated with local and regional plans.*

9. *Areas identified as having nonrenewable mineral and
aggregate resources should be planned for interim,
transitional, and "second use" utilization as well as for the
primary use.*

Try to represent more than the people who got there first.
Many of the people already living in a community realize that
additional growth has nothing for them but may destroy the
"small-town atmosphere." Ironically, they often blindly
oppose large developments where quality controls can be
applied, when actually the invisible creation of vacant lots all
over the area sets up the kind of growth that degrades an area.
The people who are dicing up the countryside are selling land
with no idea of what will be built or how and when these pieces
will fit into the community.

These lot splits and small-scale developments have been
described as the planning equivalent of stealing the horse
through the unlocked back door of the barn. One way to
preserve small-town character is to work closely with the
county to keep a semiurban mess from occurring at the fringe
between jurisdictions. An annexation and service extension
plan with teeth (no annexation, no sewers or water!) plus a
tight rein on the creation of residential building lots outside of
service areas should guide growth into areas that can be
assimilated into the existing structure of the community
without disruption.

Sewer and water projects often open the gate to runaway
unplanned growth. Many project engineers assume that
"saturation" or very high population projections justify the
favorable cost benefit ratio that depends on connection fees
and growth in assessed values. Richard Tabors said in *Rural &
Small Town Planning:*

Where suburbanization and increasing land values once were said to follow the major feeder highways into the rural countryside, now the trends appear to follow the extensions of interceptor sewers. In many existing rural communities in which on-site systems are used extensively, consideration of extension of sewers is made on the basis of septic tank failures.

While there are areas where soil characteristics are not suitable for septic systems, the more normal problem is poor maintenance and insufficiently frequent pumping. Where the alternative exists, establishment of an enforced septic tank inspection, maintenance and pumping programs can offer a cost-effective alternative to sewer extension as can actual ownership of onsite systems . . . (such as sewage authorities).[3]

[3] Richard Tabors, "Intrastructure Planning," in *Rural & Small Town Planning* (Chicago: American Planning Association, 1980). (Not copyrighted.)

Recommended Reading

Bair, Fred H., Jr. *Planning Cities*. Chicago: American Society of Planning Officials, 1970.

Bair, Fredrick H. Jr. *The Zoning Board Manual*. Chicago: APA Planners Press, 1984.

Berger, Marjorie S. ed. *Dennis O'Harrow: Plan Talk and Plain Talk*. Chicago: APA Planners Press, 1981.

Brower, David J., et al. *Managing Development in Small Towns*. Chicago: APA Planners Press, 1984.

Burchell, Robert W., and Sternlieb, George, eds. *Planning Theory in the 1980's: A Search for Future Directions*. New Brunswick, N.J.: Center for Urban Policy Research, 1979.

Catanese, Anthony J., and Snyder, James C., eds. *Introduction to Urban Planning*. New York: McGraw-Hill, 1979.

Choate, Pat and Walter, Susan. *America in Ruins: The Decaying Intrastructure*. Durham, N.C.: Duke Univ. Press, 1983.

Garnham, Henry L. *Maintaining the Spirit of Place. A Process for the Preservation of Town Character*. PDA Publishers, 1985.

Getzels, Judith and Thurow, Charles, eds. *Rural and Small Town Planning*. Chicago: APA Planners Press, 1980.

Hendler, Bruce. *Caring for the Land*. PAS #328. Chicago: American Planning Assoc, 1977.

Mater, Jean. *Public Hearings, Procedures and Strategies: A Guide to Influencing Public Decisions*. Englewood Cliffs, N.J.: Prentice-Hall, 1984.

National Trust for Historic Preservation. *Old and New Architecture: Design Relationship*. Preservation Press, 1980.

Smith, Herbert H. *The Citizens Guide to Zoning*. Chicago: APA Planners Press., 1979.

Solnit, Albert. *Project Approval*. Sylvan Press, 1983.

Stryker, Perrined. *How to Judge Environmental Planning for Subdivisions: A Citizens Guide*. Inform, Inc., 1981.

O'Mara, W. Paul. *Residential Development Handbook.* Washington, D.C.: Urban Land Institute, 1978.

Reilly, William K., ed. *The Use of Land: A Citizen's Policy Guide to Urban Growth,* Task Force Report of the Rockefeller Commission. New York: Thomas Y. Crowell Co., 1973.

Sargent, Fredrick O. *Rural Environmental Planning.* Vervana, Vt.: Author, 1976.

Tunnard, C., and Pushkarev, B. *Man-Made America: Chaos or Control?* New Haven, Conn.: Yale University Press, 1967.

Sample Rules and Regulations for a Planning Commission

Appendix A

1. The number of meetings per month and a schedule of meeting dates shall be established and may be altered or changed at any regularly scheduled meeting. Two regular meeting dates are established each month on the second and fourth Mondays at 8:00 p.m. in the Council Chambers.

2. Additional meetings may be held at any time upon the call of the chairman or by a majority of the voting members of the commission or upon request of the city council following at least twenty-four hours' notice to each member of the commission.

3. The commission at its first regular meeting In January of each year shall elect a chairman and vice-chairman and shall also elect a recording secretary who need not be an appointed member (usually the secretary is either a clerical member of the planning department staff or an employee of the commission).

4. The duties and powers of tho officers of the planning commission shall be as follows:

   A. Chairman:

   (1) Preside at all meetings of the commission.

   (2) Call special meetings of the commission in accordance with the by-laws.

   (3) Sign documents of the commission.

   (4) See that all actions of the commission are properly taken.

   B. Vice-chairman:

   During the absence, disability, or disqualification of the chairman, the vice-chairman shall exercise or perform all the duties and be subject to all the responsibilities of the chairman.

C. Recording secretary:

    (1) Keep the minutes of all meetings of the commission in an appropriate minute book.

    (2) Give or serve all notices required by law or by the by-laws.

    (3) Prepare the agenda for all meetings of the commission.

    (4) Be custodian of commission records.

    (5) Inform the commission of correspondence relating to business of the commission and attend to such correspondence.

    (6) Handle funds allocated to the commission in accordance with its directives, the law, and city regulations.

    (7) Sign official documents of the commission.

5. All maps, plats, and other matters required by law to be filed in the office of the planning department.

6. Matters referred to the commission by the city council shall be placed on the calendar for consideration and action at the first meeting of the commission after such reference.

7. A majority of the members of the commission entitled to vote shall constitute a quorum for the transaction of business.

8. Reconsideration of any decision of the commission may be had when the interested party for such reconsideration makes a showing—satisfactory to the chairman—that without fault on the part of such party essential facts were not brought to the attention of the commission.

9. *Roberts Rules of Order* are hereby adopted for the government of the commission in all cases not otherwise provided for in these rules.

10. These rules may be amended at any meeting by a vote of the majority of the entire membership of the commission provided five (5) days' notice has been given to each member of the commission.

11. Deadline for Agenda: Deadline for filing for placement on the agenda for applications for plan review and sign permits shall be twelve (12) work days prior to consideration by the plan review committee. Deadline for filing for placement on the agenda for applications for master plans, precise development plans, variances, use permits and sign variances shall be fifteen (15) working days prior to consideration by the planning commission. Requests for continuance of matters scheduled

for a particular agenda shall be filed with the planning department by Wednesday noon preceding the Monday meeting so that the printed agenda (available to the public on Friday) will reflect the requested continuance.

12. Order of Consideration of Agenda Items:

    The following procedure will normally be observed; however, it may be rearranged by the chairman for individual items if necessary for the expeditious conduct of business:

    (1) Staff presents report and makes recommendation.

    (2) The planning commission may ask questions regarding the staff presentation and report.

    (3) Proponents of the agenda items make presentation.

    (4) Any opponents make presentations.

    (5) Applicant makes rebuttal of any points not previously covered.

    (6) Planning commission asks any questions it may have of the proponents, opponents, or staff, and then takes a vote.

13. Deadline for Consideration of Agenda Items: No new agenda items shall be taken up after 12:00 p.m.

14. Designation of Voting Order: Voting to be by verbal vote; and the order of voting to be rotated each month except that the chairman shall vote last.

15. Any member of the planning commission who shall feel that he has a conflict of interest on any matter that is on the planning commission agenda shall voluntarily excuse himself, vacate his seat, and refrain from discussing and voting on said items as a planning commissioner.

16. Each member of the planning commission who has knowledge of the fact that he will not be able to attend a scheduled meeting of the planning commission shall notify the planning department at City Hall at the earliest possible opportunity and, in any event, prior to 5:00 p.m. on the date of the meeting. The planning director shall notify the chairman of the commission in the event that the projected absences will produce a lack of quorum.

17. The chairman shall be an ex officio member of all committees, with voice but no vote.

18. No member may serve two (2) full consecutive terms as chairman.

19. The vice-chairman shall succeed the chairman if he vacates his office before his term is completed, the vice-chairman to serve the unexpired term of the vacated office. A new vice-chairman shall be elected at the next regular meeting.

20. The by-laws may be amended at any meeting of the planning commission by a majority of a quorum of the commission, provided that notice of said proposed amendment is given to each member in writing at least two weeks prior to said meeting.

Sample Organization of a Planning Commission Agenda

Appendix B

General Order of Business:

1. Minutes
2. Personal appearances*
3. Scheduled matters:
   - ☐ Consent items**
   - ☐ Planned development districts
   - ☐ Public hearings
     (present policy to schedule early in evening
     if high public interest)
   - ☐ Subdivisions
   - ☐ Use permits
   - ☐ Appeals
4. Adjournment

Addressing the Planning Commission:

The public is invited to speak on any item under discussion by the planning commission, after receiving recognition by the chairman.

Please walk to any one of the microphones located at the rostrum directly in front of the commission or on stairs, and after receiving recognition from the chairman state your name and address and the purpose for appearing.

Generally speaking, the order of presentation after introduction of an item by the chairman will be:

1. Summary presentation by staff
2. Questions by the commission

169

3. Comments by the applicant
4. Comments by interested citizens
5. Additional comments by the applicant, as appropriate
6. Additional comments by staff, as necessary

At the close of the testimony, the matter will return to the planning commission for discussion and action.

Items that generate a large amount of citizen interest may be taken out of their regular position on the agenda at the discretion of the planning commission as an accommodation to the public.

* Personal Appearances

The planning commission invites citizen participation regarding the affairs of the city. Any citizen desiring to speak on a matter that is not scheduled on this agenda may do so under personal appearances at the beginning of each session. As a matter of policy, the planning commission does not take immediate action on items presented under personal appearances.

** Consent Items

Items that require little or no discussion by the planning commission, public, or applicant, are considered as "consent items," regardless of their position on the planning commission agenda. The planning commission will act on these items in one motion at the beginning of the meeting. If any concerns are expressed regarding such an item, it will be considered by the planning commission in its regular position on the agenda. **Approval by the planning commission of "consent items" means that the staff recommendation was approved together with any conditions or requirements as stated in the recommendation.** If an applicant does not plan to arrive at the beginning of the planning commission meeting, it is suggested that he phone the planning department secretary the day of the planning commission meeting to learn whether or not his item is considered to be a consent item. Those items acted upon by the planning commission as consent items will be so noted and posted near the entrance to the Council Chambers.

Sample
Environmental
Assessment Form

Appendix C

Initial Study Form Used in the City and County of San Francisco

The Environmental Assessment Form is to be used for the federal environmental review of all non-exempt projects proposed in the Community Development Block Grant Program. The environmental review process must be completed prior to the request for the release of funds for the project.

The environmental assessment conducted by the applicant will determine the environmental impact of any proposed project, note any necessary changes that would eliminate or minimize adverse impacts, and assess the appropriate level of environmental clearance. If through the environmental review process the applicant concludes that the proposed project should not be implemented, based on environmental considerations, the applicant may terminate or abandon the project.

The first four pages of this form are to be filled out by the applicant, the rest will be completed by the Department of City Planning.

I. General Information:

Project Title:

Project Location — Specific:

Project Location — City: County:

Description of Nature, Purpose and Beneficiaries of Project:

Name of Person, Board, Commission or Department proposing to carry out project:

A. List and describe any other related permits and other public approvals required for this project, including those required by City, regional, state, and other federal agencies:

B. Existing zoning district:

Present use of site:

C. Proposed use of site (project for which this form is filed):

II. Project description:

A. Describe the type of project and the project's physical characteristics, including:

1. Site size.

2. Square footage.

3. Number of floors of construction.

4. Amount of off-street parking provided.

5. Submit plans.

6. Proposed scheduling.

7. Associated projects.

8. Anticipated incremental development.

9. If residential, include the number of units, schedule of unit sizes, range of sale prices or rents, and type of household and household size expected.

10. If commercial, indicate the type, whether neighborhood or city oriented, square footage of sales area, and loading facilities.

11. If industrial, indicate the type, estimated employment per shift, and loading facilites.

12. If institutional, indicate the major function, estimated employment per shift, estimated occupancy, loading facilities, and community benefits to be derived from the project.

13. If the project involves a variance, conditional use or rezoning application, state this and indicate clearly why the application is required. Any such application required for the project must be filed with the Department of City Planning before action is taken on the Environmental Evaluation.

B. Are the following items applicable to the project or its effects?

1. Change in existing features of any bays, tidelands, beaches, lakes or hills, or substantial alteration of ground contours.

2. Change in scenic views or vistas from existing residential areas or public lands or roads.

3. Change in pattern, scale or character of general area of project.

4. Significant effect on plant or animal life.

5. Significant amounts of solid waste or litter.

6. Change in dust, ash, smoke, fumes or odors in vicinity.

7. Change in ocean, bay, lake, stream or ground water quality or quanitity, or alteration of existing drainage patterns.

8. Change in existing noise or vibration levels in the vicinity.

9. Site on filled land or on slope of 10 per cent or more.

10. Use or disposal of potentially hazardous materials, such as toxic substances, flammables or explosives.

11. Change in demand for City services (police, fire, water, sewage, etc.).

12. Increased fossil fuel consumption (electricity, oil, natural gas, etc.).

13. Relationship to a larger project or series of projects.

III. Determine Existing Conditions:

A. Describe the *project site* as it exists before the project, including information on topography, soil stability, plants and animals, and any scenic aspects. Describe any existing structures on the site and the use of the structures.

B. Describe the *surrounding properties*, including information on plants and animals and any scenic aspects. Indicate the type of land use (residential, commercial, etc.), intensity of land use (one-family, apartment houses, shops, department stores, etc.), and scale of development (height, frontage, set-back, rear yard, etc.).

C. Describe any known cultural, historical or archeological aspects of the existing site and surrounding area. List properties on National Register or eligible for inclusion on this list.

IV. Identification of Environmental Impacts:

1. Is the project in conflict with environmental plans and goals that have been adopted by the community where the project is to be located?

2. Is the project controversial in the community where the project is to be located?

3. Does the project have a substantial and demonstrable negative aesthetic effect?

4. Does the project substantially affect a rare or endangered species of animal or plant, or habitat of such a species?

173

5. Does the project cause substantial interference with the movement of any resident or migratory fish or wildlife species?

6. Does the project breach any published national, state or local standards relating to solid waste or litter control?

7. Does the project result in a substantial detrimental effect on air or water quality, or on ambient noise levels for adjoining areas?

8. Does the project involve the possibility of contaminating a public water supply system or adversely affecting ground water?

9. Could the project cause substantial flooding, erosion or siltation?

10. Could the project expose people or structures to major geologic hazards?

11. Could the project affect any site listed or eligible for listing on the National Register?

12. Other factors or significant secondary consequences (specify).

Mandatory Findings of Significance:

1. Does the project have the potential to degrade the quality of the environment, or curtail the range of the environment?

2. Does the project have the potential to achieve short-term, to the disadvantage of long-term, environmental goals? (A short-term impact on the environment is one which occurs in a relatively brief, definitive period of time while long-term impacts will endure well into the future.)

3. Does the project have impacts which are individually limited, but cumulatively considerable? (A project may impact on two or more separate resources where the impact on each resource is relatively small, but where the effect of the total of those impacts on the environment is significant.)

4. Does the project substantially affect a rare or endangered species of animal or plant, or habitat of such a species?

5. Does the project have the potential to be controversial?

V. Examination of Identified Impacts:

A. Possible Project Modifications:

Examine the project and consider ways in which the project or external factors relating to the project could be modified in order to eliminate or minimize any adverse environmental impacts and protect or enhance environmental quality. The examination should include consideration in light of policies set forth in NEPA, of both positive and negative effects of any such modification in relation to design, use, location, cost and timing the proposed project and its implementation. All appropriate means should be undertaken to assure that any environmentally desirable conditions and safeguards are implemented.

B. Alternative Projects:

Examine alternatives to the project which would eliminate or minimize environmental impacts or enhance environmental quality. The examination should include consideration of both positive and negative effects of any such alternatives in relation to design, use, location, cost and time, and consideration of the effect of no project.

Project Checklist

Appendix D

(This checklist was developed by the Department of Urban Planning, University of Oregon, 1975.)

	Proposed Project		
NATURAL/PHYSICAL	**Are the Following Affected**		
Land Use	Yes	Positively	Negatively
Alteration of unique features			
Unstable soil conditions			
Alteration of drainage patterns			
Creation of impervious surfaces			
Construction of barriers			
Use of agricultural land			
Construction on steep slopes			
Construction on flood plains			
Change in existing land-use patterns			
Impact on plant and animal life			
Stimulation of additional land use by related activities			
Pollution			
Dust, fumes, smoke, or odors			
Increased auto emissions			
Geographic features affecting air quality			
Effects on local climate			
Change in noise levels			
Application or disposal of pesticides or herbicides			
Use and disposal of toxic chemicals			
Solid waste generation			
Sedimentation or pollutants introduced to water supply			
Changes in possible radiation sources			
Resource Use			
Blasting and drilling			
Surface excavation			

NATURAL/PHYSICAL	Proposed Project Are the Following Affected		
Land Use	Yes	Positively	Negatively
Subsurface excavation			
Well drilling and fluid removal			
Clear-cutting and other vegetation removal			
Commercial fishing and hunting			
Grazing activity			
Water supply			
Effect on long-term supply or sustained yield			
Potential for recycling activity			
Substantial energy demands			
Ecosystem			
Exotic flora and fauna			
Modification of food supply			
Introduction of pollutants			
Predator control			
Introduction of new species			
Water quality			
Breeding or nesting places for wildlife or fish			
COMMUNITY AND REGIONAL IMPACTS			
Residential density			
Commercial activity			
Retail/entertainment facilities			
Industrial development and facilities			
Transportation facilities and convenience			
Availability and adequacy of public services			
Sewage capacity			
Water, gas, and electricity demand and supply			
Solid waste disposal			
Public safety and fire protection			
Growth-inducing impacts			
Effect on relationships among public agencies			
SOCIOECONOMIC IMPACT			
Social			
Substantial population changes			
Change in number of families or family size			

177

NATURAL/PHYSICAL Land Use	Proposed Project Are the Following Affected		
	Yes	Positively	Negatively
Alteration of age, income, or racial mix			
Housing type and quality			
Housing density and number			
Change in land and housing costs			
Displacement—people or families			
Urban design characteristics			
Modification of social fabric or community structure			
Historical or traditional qualities			
Visual qualities of an area or site			
Opportunities for socializing			
Cultural opportunities			
Recreational facilities/ playgrounds			
Effects that may cause stress or negative mental experiences			
Possibility for criminal activity			
Convenience of public and private services			
Compatibility with existing community policies			
Alteration of government structure or responsiveness			
Economic			
Effect on basic economy			
Effect on existing firms, industries, or centers of economic activity			
Employment income opportunities			
Substantial public expenditures			
Change in taxation			
Excessive burdening of a particular group or sector			
Growth-inducing effects			
Adequacy of necessary local resources			
Short-term energy availability and cost			
Long-term energy availability and cost			
Relation to changing technologies			
Relation to changes in regional, national, and international economic structures			

An Anatomy of the Classic Southwestern Land Fraud Scheme

Appendix E

There are many variations of fraudulent land sales schemes. This type of fraud may occur not only in the sale of the land itself, but also in the financing of the land sales company. In fact, the greater damage is usually done through the investment aspect of the land fraud which may be a securities fraud. This hypothetical is based on a composite of various aspects of major land fraud schemes. This outline of the methods and techniques utilized by land fraud promoters is offered so that purchasers, financial institutions, attorneys for subdividers, and government officials involved in the regulation of land development ventures will recognize their characteristics, detect them early, and avoid them.

1. *The land purchase stage: The early stages of land fraud usually involve a well-organized plan to acquire remote grazing land in large quantities with very little money being paid down. The primary characteristic here is a developer or promoter with very little initial capital of his own who, from the beginning, never really intends to fully develop the subdivision or to make it work. The subdivision can be created on a reverse cash flow basis with income and capital generated solely from the real estate contracts of purchasers.*

   The promoter may begin by contacting a rancher and buying a large amount of land acreage with very little down payment. Additional land may then be tied up on an option basis. The rancher is allowed to foreclose on the entire subdivision if his monthly payment under the real estate contract is not met. Thus, for a few thousand dollars down a promoter can tie up thousands of acres of land. The rancher agrees to sell land typically valued at only $50 dollars an acre for grazing purposes at $100 dollars an acre to a developer under an agreement to release the acreage to the developer at the rate of $100 dollars an acre.

2. **Real estate trust stage:** The sale of the land to the public is usually accomplished through a complicated two or three beneficiary trust arrangement designed to disguise the large number of prior lienholders on the property from the purchaser and his attorney. The trustee is usually a title company or escrow bank which may have a secure sounding name. Payments made under the real estate contracts are sent to the trustee who divides up the proceeds and pays the many beneficiaries of the trust who are usually: (1) the rancher, (2) a banker who lends money to the promoter under a mortgage, and (3) the promoter himself. A key characteristic of a land fraud situation is that the contracts themselves are not held in an escrow account by the trustee nor are the contract payments sent directly to the trustee by the third-party purchasers. The contracts may be held by the promoter, or a company owned by the promoter, who intercepts the monthly payments under the contract by having the purchaser send his payments to a central collection company which he controls. The advantage of controlling the contracts and the collections by utilizing a central collection company is important in what may become the second stage of the fraud — the selling of the contracts themselves on assignment to third-party investors.

3. **The advertising and sales organizations stage:** Once the land has been subdivided by the promoter and local subdivision regulations have been complied with and plats filed, the promoter usually concentrates on advertising and promoting the sale of the land. A considerable amount of money may be expended to develop sales techniques and promotional materials for selected areas of the country. Usually these sales areas are in distant parts of the country where the prospective purchasers are uninformed about the land values or characteristics of the land in the Southwest. However, the same techniques described below are being used more and more in all metropolitan market areas, even those cities in the Southwest located near the subdivisions. Frequently, sales are made in cold northern states during the winter months where the land sold may be promoted as a new retirement community with low taxes at affordable prices. The one or two thousand dollars per acre price may appear to be a bargain to prospective purchasers living in urban or farm

areas who are used to much greater land values. It may be inconceivable to them that the land itself may have virtually little or no value in terms of any type of residential use.

Promotions are often made at dinners or mass meetings under high-pressure sales conditions where prospective buyers are shown colorful graphs with land values ever increasing, and where the purchasers are made to believe that the land is selling fast and that they must buy now to insure reserving a good parcel. Often the sales are made with money-back guarantees and all-expense-paid trips to see the land before the sale is finalized. Later the purchaser may discover that the trip is free only if he decides to buy the land once he has arrived on location or only if he agrees to buy additional property. The trips are typically planned well in advance and the promoter may even erect temporary buildings or hire road graders and part-time employees to work on these "visit" weekends to convey the impression to purchasers that the subdivision is under construction. Flags, mock utility poles, or pipes may be scattered around the subdivision so that purchasers are conned into thinking that the construction of all the promised utilities and recreational facilities is in progress. The key characteristic here is that none of the promised utilities (i.e., water lines, tennis courts, sewer systems, swimming pool, roads, golf courses) may ever really be completed. They always remain in a "planning stage" or "under construction."

The land is pitched as a "good investment" that can be resold at a profit at a later date. Purchasers may be shown rigged appraisals and are told to buy now at a much reduced price. Purchasers may typically be told that land is one thing "they don't make any more of." Purchasers are not told that the land value is already grossly inflated either by less than arm's-length transactions between companies owned by the promoter, the promoter's expensive promotion and advertising costs, or the promoter's desire to make grossly excessive profits. They are also not told that the land usually has no local resale market and that the developer himself has a large or unlimited inventory of lots with which the purchaser must later compete when he decides to resell his land. Often the sales take place in the purchaser's house where the salesman appeals to the husband's investment instincts and family protector image.

Another key characteristic of a land fraud situation is the use of "free-lance" real estate agents who are given unusually high sales commissions. Some are allowed up to 30% for the sale of undeveloped land. Thus, such real estate agents have a tremendous incentive to get the purchaser to put in as much cash as possible as a down payment, from which the agent takes his commission. They also may have the incentive to promise everything and anything under the sun just to make the sale. The contract usually contains a "merger clause" disclaiming any oral representation made by the salesman. Such a clause may often be hidden in the fine print of the contract. The promoter is able to later disclaim these oral representations because the salesman is not an employee or an agent of the company. In fraudulent land developments the promoter is more interested in the consummated real estate contract, which he can later sell at a discount on assignment, than he is in receiving the down payment or having a solid contract that will produce monthly payments in the future over the full life of the contract. Thus, what happens is that salesmen usually go to great lengths to develop their own advertising materials and techniques that may be repleat with misrepresentations and worthless guarantees that will never be honored.

4. **The paper-sale stage:** By this time in a fraudulant land scheme, the promoter may have a serious reverse cash flow problem. He has paid money to buy the land, to initially develop it, and to pay for the advertising materials, appraisals, and surveys. Most of the down payments are being taken by the salesmen as commissions. All the developer has are the contracts and promises of future monthly payments. Most legitimate land developers have planned for this eventuality. They have sufficient capitalization to carry them until the contracts begin to pay off over the long run. The illegitimate operation is usually undercapitalized and the promoters must resort to a "Ponzi"-type scheme to make their money up front and fast before the development is exposed and eventually collapses. Therefore, the next step in the fraud may be a fraudulent securities situation. To make money, the promoter may now attempt to sell, at a discount on assignment, the land purchase contracts. A network of paper sales organizations are set up around the country similar to the network of real estate salesmen which has been set up to sell the land. Small investors are contacted by brokers and salesmen and offered the chance to buy a real estate contract at a substantial discount. The investors may be guaranteed up to a 20% to

30% return on their investment taking into account the discount. They are also promised that if the contract turns out to be bad it will be replaced with another contract of similar value. Again, the salesmen are given substantial commissions which they take from the down payment, and they have every incentive to misrepresent the risks involved and the future development of the subdivision. The contract purchaser who invests may be promised that as a security he can foreclose on the land itself if he does not get paid by the land purchaser. The investor may never be given a true picture of the property, its value, or the number of other prior lienholders who have mortgages on the property.

The "Ponzi" nature of the scheme comes into play next. The investors who buy the contracts and the land purchaser on the contract may never meet or know of each other because all payments are sent to the promoter's collection company by the purchaser and mailed from that same collection company to the investor. The company may thus be able to cover up defaults with other land purchaser's payments. Eventually, as the contracts start to go bad and people discover the true character of the subdivision, it is difficult to find more purchasers to buy the subdivided land. In order to continue to sell contracts at a discount to investors, the promoter may resort to a device called "fence posting." Phoney contracts are signed by salesmen or even drunks in bars, and then sold at a discount to eager investors who by now have been receiving a good return on their money and want to buy more "paper."

As a final end step in this stage of the fraud the promoter may take out large loans from banks or small lending institutions and use as collateral the land itself or other accounts receivable generated by the land contracts which may or may not have already been assigned or sold to other investors. The promoter may attempt to keep the project afloat as long as possible, pocketing as much of the up-front money generated from the sale of the contracts, the land, and from the loans as he possibly can. Typically, he may never invest any of this money in the development of the subdivision.

5. **The undertaker stage:** Eventually when the time is right and the development has been milked for all it can, the promoter may "call in the undertaker" in the words of the trade. The corporation is placed in receivership or bankruptcy is declared. Another variation may be to sell the land

development to an unsuspecting businessman who is unaware of the problems with the land purchase contracts. The business may even be sold to a "professional" who then proceeds to loot the corporation of all remaining assets before taking it through bankruptcy.

6. **The collapse and the victims:** Once the collapse takes place and bankruptcy is declared, the law enforcement agencies, the courts, and the creditors may be left with an incredible morass of overlapping claims by creditors, banks, landowners, and defrauded purchasers of the land contracts. The land purchaser may not get title to the land or a refund of any of his money. The rancher is left with land which is tied up in litigation by foreclosing creditors and with title to the property indefinitely clouded by liens and various interests held by purchasers. This may result in the checkerboarding of the whole area of land, thus preventing any later consolidation or return of the land to agricultural or grazing use. The banks and investors who purchase the contracts are left with worthless paper and valueless land as a security with only the meaningless legal right to either foreclose on the property or sue the land purchaser. The fallout effect of such frauds can be monumental. In one major land fraud venture of this type in Arizona, the promoters were estimated to have made $11.8 million over a three-year period based on 2,000 acres of land purchased by the promoter with only an initial investment of $10,000. The bankruptcy left $8 million in unsecured debts.[1]

---

[1] State of New Mexico, Office of the Attorney General, *Land Fraud and Consumer Protection Laws and Remedies* (Santa Fe, 1980).

Example of a Report on a Quasi-Judicial Action with Facts, Findings, and Recommendations[1]

Appendix F

I. Facts

  A. General Information

    Proposal: Zone Change from A2.5 to M3.

    Location: 4735 S.W. Beaverton-Hillsdale Highway.

    Neighborhood: Bridlemile

    Legal Description: Lot 27, Block 8, Fairvale.

    Zones: A2.5 to M3.

    Petition Percentage: 88 percent.

    Description of Plan: To use the site for "general purposes." The plot plan indicates the conversion of the existing dwelling on the site to an office. The applicant indicates 1,861 square feet in the house. The first and second floors would be used for office purposes with storage in the basement.

  B. Site Information

    Site Description: This 5,817.5-square-feet site is developed with a single-family dwelling already converted to office use. The site slopes down to the north with the northern portion of the site approximately 15 feet below the southern portion of the site abutting S.W. Beaverton-Hillsdale Highway. The southern portion of the site, between the house and office and S.W. Beaverton-Hillsdale Highway, has been recently paved with blacktop. The blacktop extends to the west in front (south) of the applicant's duplex next door.

---

[1] From City of Portland, Oregon, Hearings Officer report to the City Planning Commission.

C. Vicinity Data

Surrounding Conditions: To the north is an electrical substation zoned M3 with single-family dwellings zoned R7 and some multifamily units zoned A2.5 farther north. To the west is the applicant's duplex with scattered development on the north side of S.W. Beaverton-Hillsdale Highway. To the south are single-family dwellings and some multifamily units zoned R7 and A2.5. Immediately to the east is dedicated alley and an area of gravel and cut logs. Farther east is a Frame Shop. To the east along the Highway are various commercial businesses on both sides of the street.

Service Considerations: Urban services have been installed in this area. S.W. Beaverton-Hillsdale Highway is a four-lane state highway and designated as a Major Traffic and Transit Street according to the Arterial Streets Policy.

D. Agencies Contacted

City Engineer, Traffic Engineer, Fire Bureau, Water Engineer, Bureau of Neighborhood Environment, Bureau of Buildings, Tri-Met, Neighborhood Planning, Transportation Planning, State Highway Department, and Bridlemile-Robert Gray Neighborhood Association.

E. Exhibits (Numbers 1 through 5 refer to exhibits originally part of the Planning Staff Report. When unnecessary to this Report, they are not attached.)

1 — Applicant's Statement (not attached)
2 — Vicinity Map
3 — Zoning Map
4 — Land-Use Map (not attached)
5 — Transportation Planning Response (not attached)

II. Findings

A. Code Consideratons: A2.5, low-density apartment zone, permits one unit per 2,500 square feet of site area with a minimum lot size of 5,000 square feet. A duplex would be the maximum A2.5 density permitted on this site.

M3, light manufacturing zone, permits single-family dwellings, apartments (three units in this case), commercial and light industrial uses. Offices are permitted in an M3 zone. Off-street parking is required at the ratio of one space per 700 square feet of gross floor area. The applicant indicates 1,861 square feet of floor area for the office use which requires three parking spaces. The house at the time of the field inspection was occupied as an office.

The newly installed pavement appears to serve the duplex (two parking spaces required) as well as the office. The parking spaces have not been lined (painted), but there appears to be adequate room for the five required off-street parking spaces.

B. Agency Responses

The *City Engineer* comments, "The Oregon State Highway Department has control of Beaverton-Hillsdale Highway at this location and should be consulted concerning street access. A sanitary sewer is available north of north property line; easement would be required. Storm water must be directed to a suitable disposal point in a manner satisfactory to the City Engineer."

The *Bureau of Buildings* notes that storm water disposal is a problem in this area.

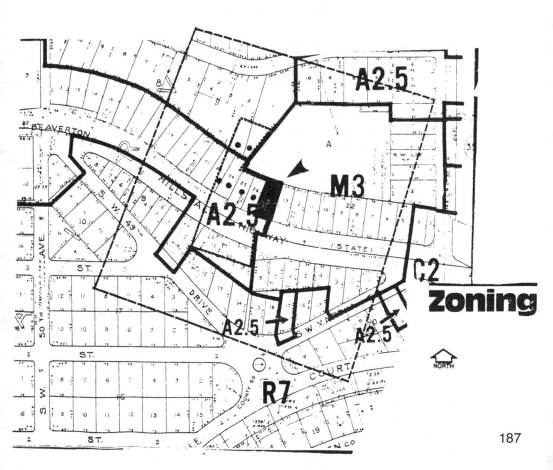

The *Bridlemile-Robert Gray Neighborhood Association* has not responded.

C. Land Use Inventory Considerations: According to the 1976 land-use inventory, there were 7.75 acres of A2.5-zoned land with 3.2 acres vacant. There were 5.9 acres of M3-zoned land with 3.4 acres vacant.

D. There are a number of facets to this case, many of which point in different directions.

E. The difficulties which the site history shows between the applicant and Bureau of Buildings as to appropriate occupancy of the site can be resolved most easily, and most advantageously to the applicant, by the allowance of office use on the site.

F. There is not likely to be any enhanced neighborhood impact from office use available through rezoning as compared to the potential for duplex use under current zoning.

G. The combined use of one access by this site and the site immediately west will reduce the number of curb cuts needed to serve adjacent properties along Beaverton-Hillsdale. That has already been accomplished by the applicant.

H. Despite these apparent advantages to rezoning, there is a real problem attendant to changing this zone from A2.5 to M3. It enlarges the size of the only industrial zoning in this area along Beaverton-Hillsdale. And it begins a westward march of that industrial zone expansion along the Highway. It is noted here that all of the owners of land west of this site within the petition area have signed the petition. That at least indicates a potential for further requests of westward expansion of the industrial zone. Such strip industrial zoning along Beaverton-Hillsdale would appear most unfortunate.

I. There has been a recent Council decision which refused an extension of commercial strip zoning in this neighborhood at the intersection of S.W. 51st Avenue and Beaverton-Hillsdale Highway (P.C. File No. 6639).

J. It is possible, however, that all of these discordant needs can be met by declining the zone change but allowing a Revocable Permit on this site for office use. This will effectively stymie any further expansion of the industrial zoning pattern. It will allow the applicant's intended use while not impacting the neighborhood. And it will clearly serve as discouragement to others who might seek to expand the industrial zone in this area.

III. Conclusions

These facts and findings fail to support a conclusion that there is a public need for an expansion of the industrial zone in this area. However, these facts and findings do support the allowance of a Revocable Permit on this site for office use subject to appropriate landscaping conditions.

IV. Recommendation

It is therefore the recommendation of the Hearings Officer that the zone change from A2.5 to M3 be denied, but that a Revocable Permit for office purposes be allowed, subject to the following conditions:

A. Parking for this site as well as the applicant's property to the west shall be lined and improved as required per Chapter 33.82.

B. Storm water shall be managed per City Engineer and Bureau of Buildings Plumbing Division specifications.

C. A detailed landscaping plan shall be submitted to the Bureau of Planning for review and approval prior to the issuance of an occupancy permit. That landscaping plan shall include appropriate screening of the parking lots and buffering of the site from the highway.

Some Relevant Questions About You and Your Planning Commission

Appendix G

A. Does your planning agency have . . . (if not, do you know why not?) **Basic tools and procedures**	Response (percent)		Notes
	yes	no	
1. An up-to-date *general plan* (revised and adopted within the past three years)?	61	39	
2. General plan *documents and maps* readily available to the public?	86	14	
3. An "adequate" general plan?	73	27	"Adequate" refers to meeting legal requirements for general plans in a particular state.
4. A *zoning map* prominently displayed at the zoning counter and in the room in which you hold commission meetings?	71	29	
5. Zoning maps available to hand out?	72	28	
6. An up-to-date *existing land-use map*?	65	35	
7. A published set of specific *action programs* to implement the goals and policies of the general plan?	59	41	

		Yes	No	Notes
8. A professionally trained planning staff *that also* keeps up to date through continuing education and retraining?		79	21	
9. A *procedure* for regular reconsideration and review of its general plan and implementation devices (zoning ordinances, etc.)?		70	30	
10. Projects regularly referred to it by other agencies (as required by law)?		83	17	
11. A procedure for reviewing and acting on referrals from city departments and other agencies, as required by state law?		85	15	
B. Have you ever . . . **Job behavior**		**Yes**	**No**	**Notes**
1. Voted yes on a proposed zone change or other such proposal when you really wanted to vote no?		42	58	
2. Been intimidated by staff and thus essentially at their mercy, or immobilized?		5	95	
3. Been intimidated by an applicant?		42	58	
4. Criticized your staff when they misperformed or disappointed you?		65	35	

5. Had a study session with your staff to go over procedures and matters of commission-staff relations and procedures (as distinguished from matters associated with agenda items)?	61	39
6. Had a meeting with your city (or county) attorney to discuss legal powers and limitations, the jurisdiction's planning laws, etc?	60	40
7. Had a meeting with a neighboring city or the county planning commission to discuss common problems?	60	40
8. Met as a body jointly for study session purposes with your own city council (or county board of supervisors)?	66	34
9. Held a *public forum* to ask citizens what they want of you and of the planning program for their community (not a public hearing on a specific issue, but an open nonagenda function)?	33	67
10. Read a book about planning or cities?	77	23
11. Felt the planning commission was impotent or of no value (e.g., usually overruled)?	27	73

12. Represented the planning commission before the city council (or county board of supervisors) as an advocate of a specific planning commission position?	47	53	
13. Lobbied in the community for a planning commission proposal you believed in?	46	54	
14. Been asked to review the proposed budget for the planning department?	60	40	
15. Participated in developing an annual work program for the planning agency?	59	41	
16. *Seen* a work program for the agency?	54	46	It's interesting to note that 5 percent more of the respondents have participated in developing a work program than have actually seen one!
17. Talked or agreed among your associates about the procedures followed in conducting meetings and public hearings?	85	15	
18. Been given a "lesson" by your staff on the importance of "making findings" before making decisions, and how to do so?	72	28	
19. Participated in hiring a consultant?	33	67	

20. Videotaped a commission meeting and viewed yourself in action as commissioners?	13	87	
21. Felt you had become almost totally dependent upon your staff for ideas and the bases for making decisions?	30	70	
22. Felt decisions sometimes are made almost entirely on the basis of the strength of proponent or opponent (best debator won)?	39	61	
23. Felt you wanted to complain to the city (or county) manager or the city council (or county board of supervisors) about the performance or behavior of your staff planners?	24	76	
24. Said, "We don't know and we're not ready to make a decision. Let's question or think awhile about everything before us and make no decision until we know what we are doing"?	60	40	

194

Author's Note

And, finally, if all this leaves the reader feeling that there's too much to do, here are some simple techniques for "how to avoid action":

1. For every proposal, set up an opposite and then "concede" to a "middle ground" (no action at all).

2. Profess not to have the answer (this lets you out of having any answer at all)—while earnestly cautioning against proceeding too rapidly (which helps avoid ever getting started).

3. Emphasize righteously that "this problem cannot be separated from other related problems." (Translation: We can't solve this problem until we have solved all related problems—which means never.)

4. Ask what is meant by the question. (By the time this is explained to the satisfaction of even a small minority, it is time to go home.)

5. Earnestly caution the gathering that "we had better wait until we can consult an expert!" or, as an equally effective action-stopper: "Let's appoint a committee!"

6. In closing, be sure to congratulate the problem. "It has stimulated discussion, contributed to growth, opened new vistas, and shown us the way." (We may have wasted two perfectly good hours, but that problem surely deserves a medal.)[1]

---

[1] From the *San Francisco Examiner*, November 3, 1973.

Index